AZ PUZZLE BOOK

Published by Collins
An imprint of HarperCollins Publishers
Westerhill Road
Bishopbriggs
Glasgow G64 2QT
collins.reference@harpercollins.co.uk
www.harpercollins.co.uk

First published 2019

Puzzles by Gareth Moore

A catalogue record for this book is available from the British Library

ISBN 978-0-00835175-5

10 9 8 7 6 5 4 3 2 1

Printed in Slovenia

MIX
Paper from
responsible sources
FSC™ C007454

CONTENTS

HISTORY OF A-Z

It's impossible to think of the iconic A-Z and not think about our founder, Phyllis Pearsall, or Mrs P as she was always affectionately known. Those of us who had the privilege of spending time with her (she always had time for everyone) could see that here was a rather extraordinary woman. Her own journey is an incredible story in itself, and it was with great spirit and determination that, over 80 years ago, the first *London A-Z* came into being.

We were founded in 1936 by her father, Alexander Grosz, who had come to London from Hungary in 1900 seeking his fortune. There he met Isabelle (Bella) Crowley in a creamery near Elephant and Castle. Despite resistance from her family, the couple married 2 years later in Gretna Green and soon had two children, Anthony (Tony) and Phyllis.

The couple established their first map company, Geographia Ltd, in 1908 and so began Alexander's 50 years in the mapping business. The company grew quickly, and after the outbreak of the First World War they regularly produced war maps for *The Telegraph,* with whom they had built up a good relationship. With this increase in business, the family moved out of London to Claygate.

After 17 years, Alexander and Bella's marriage came to an end in 1920. Bella began divorce proceedings, and in response, Alexander removed her as a director of Geographia Ltd. This proved to be a tough time for Alexander – he authorized the purchase of the printing company Gilbert Whitehead by Geographia Ltd, and then the production of a World Atlas. The first edition sold well, but a second and third printing didn't sell. Following on from this, Alexander was voted off Geographia's board and moved to Chicago where he began teaching English. The company was later sold to the bank for a paltry £1,000.

At this time, Phyllis had no place in London to call home so she took a position at the Collège de Jeunes Filles in Fécamp, France, both as a pupil and a teacher and then later trained as an artist at the Sorbonne in Paris. Her brother, Tony, spent some time studying at the Slade, and then the École Des Beaux-Arts, both famous art colleges. It was during a visit to him that Phyllis first met his friend, Richard Pearsall. The two were married in 1926, and they were to spend many of their years together travelling, initially around Belgium, and then on to Spain, mostly for the warmer climate.

In 1936, Phyllis returned to London without Richard, and her father set her up with the company that still stands today. The newly formed organization had its first offices in Napier House, 24-27 High Holborn. The first publication to go on sale was Alexander's *Map Of The World*, with the plan to produce three London publications, including the *OK* atlas. The first maps were created by Phyllis walking the streets of London, although the initial title of *OK Maps* was changed at the last minute to *A to Z*.

During the Second World War, street maps that the company had created were withdrawn from sale. Taking the lead from her father, Phyllis found work for the business producing war maps for the newspapers, and she also worked as an artist painting images of women working in the war effort. The restriction was dropped in 1944 and our maps went immediately back into production.

In 1962, the business moved down to Kent where we are still based to this date. With Phyllis acutely aware of her own mortality, and with her overriding concern for the welfare of the staff, her thoughts turned to what would become of the company in the event of her death. She was keen that the business should not be taken out of the hands of those that had helped to build it so she took the extraordinary step of placing the ownership of the business into a trust. Therefore, in 1965, the Geographers' Map Trust was created, and both her and Tony's shares were purchased by the trust for £10,000 and £50,000 respectively.

By the end of the '60s, Fred Bond had taken on the role of Joint Managing Director, and the company flourished under his steady hand. The 'A-Z' was then added to the company name in 1973, despite having been an integral part of the map title since the very beginning.

Phyllis was awarded an MBE in 1986, also the 50th year of the company. With strong sales, and a solid management team, the business thrived, building success upon success for many years. In 1992, the company moved to brand new premises in Borough Green, designed to the requirements of A-Z.

It was shortly after celebrating the 60th anniversary of A-Z at Disneyland Paris, and 28 days short of her 90th birthday, that Phyllis passed away. Her spirit, however, is still very much alive and with us as we continue in a very different mapping world to the one the business was born into all those years ago. Mapping methods have changed significantly, yet our approach to detail and accuracy has never wavered.

A-Z TIMELINE

1879 – Alexander Grosz born in Csurog, Austria-Hungary (now part of Serbia).

1885 – Isabelle Crowley (Bella) born.

1903 – Alexander marries Bella in Gretna Green.

1905 – Anthony (Tony) Gross is born.

1906 – Phyllis Isobella Gross born 25 September.

1908 – Alexander and Bella found Geographia Ltd.

1915 – With increasing income from war maps, the Gross family move to Claygate.

1918 – Alexander is granted The Freedom of the City of London.

1920 – Bella starts divorce proceedings, and Alexander removes her as a director of Geographia. Alexander buys a printing company, Gilbert Whitehead, and produces a World Atlas, but the 2nd and 3rd printings sell badly. Geographia Ltd votes to remove Alexander from the board. Geographia Ltd is purchased for £1,000 by the bank.

1921 – Alexander moves to Chicago and teaches English. Phyllis takes a position at the Collège de Jeunes Filles at Fécamp as a pupil/teacher. Tony attends the Slade and studies at the École Des Beaux-Arts. Phyllis meets Tony's friend, Richard Pearsall.

1936 – Alexander sets up Geographers' Map Company in London on 25 August.

1940 – London maps are withdrawn from sale due to government orders, but the business is busy producing war maps.

1944 – The government order restricting map sales is revoked.

1947 – First company van purchased.

1954 – Tony becomes Art Director of Geographers'.

1965 – Plans for a trust are put together. The company shares are valued at £82,500. The initial trust is set up.

1973 – A-Z added to the company name on 15 May.

1982 – Anthony Gross is awarded a CBE.

1986 – The company celebrates its 50th Anniversary on the Thames. Phyllis is awarded an MBE.

1996 – Phyllis stands down as Chairman. The business celebrates the 60th Anniversary at Disneyland Paris. Phyllis passes away 28 August.

2012 – A-Z are selected to be the official map publisher of the 2012 London Olympics.

2013 – The original trust hands over the business to a new 2013 Trust in August.

2016 – We celebrate our 80 years.

HOW TO USE THIS BOOK

We have carefully selected each of the maps in this book for a specific reason: some capture an iconic location, others a significant moment in history or a place of sporting glory. Grouped into sections including History, Sport, Entertainment, Transport and Nature, each map is accompanied by a description of the site and a puzzle that will challenge you to unlock the secrets of Britain's streets.

One thing it's very important to remember as you pit your wits against the street map experts is that any words or locations that occur in the yellow area of the map do not count, and will not feature, as part of an answer unless specifically stated in the question.

All of the puzzles will test your knowledge of the map, but they are organized into three areas. **It's on the Map** will ask you to find specific locations, **Cryptic Challenges** will invite you to solve a cryptic puzzle and **The Knowledge** will test your general knowledge.

This book takes a fresh and interesting look at our maps and shows how much change is a part of our lives. We hope that by looking through these puzzles you will gain some insight into the work that is involved in creating the maps behind them and be inspired to see them in a new light and with new interest.

As Mrs P was fond of saying, 'On we go'!

AZ®
PUZZLES

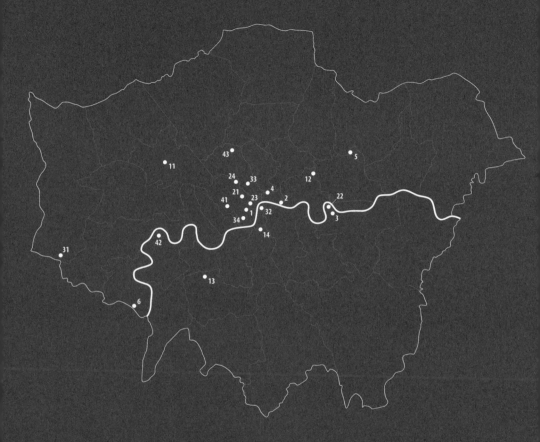

1. Buckingham Palace
2. Tower of London
3. Greenwich
4. The Oldest Terraced Houses in London
5. City of London Cemetery
6. Hampton Court Palace
11. Wembley
12. Queen Elizabeth Olympic Park
13. Wimbledon
14. The Oval
21. Oxford Street

22. O$_2$ Arena
23. London's West End
24. London Zoo
31. Heathrow Airport
32. Waterloo
33. Euston/King's Cross
34. Victoria Coach Station
41. Hyde Park
42. Royal Botanic Gardens at Kew
43. Hampstead Heath

7. Hastings
8. Cambridge City Centre
9. Caerphilly Castle
10. Edinburgh Castle
15. Cheltenham Racecourse
16. Rugby
17. Loughborough University
18. Cardiff Arms Park
19. Celtic Park/Sir Chris Hoy Velodrome
20. St Andrews
25. Harry Potter Studio Tour
26. Royal Shakespeare Theatre
27. Glastonbury
28. Chester Zoo
29. Blackpool

30. Kelvingrove Museum
35. Portsmouth Harbour
36. Dover
37. Birmingham New Street
38. M6/M42 Junction
39. Sheffield Supertram
40. Mancunian Way
44. Preston Park
45. Wollaton Park
46. Sefton Park
47. Windermere
48. Saltwell Park
49. Town Moor
50. Holyrood Park

HISTORY

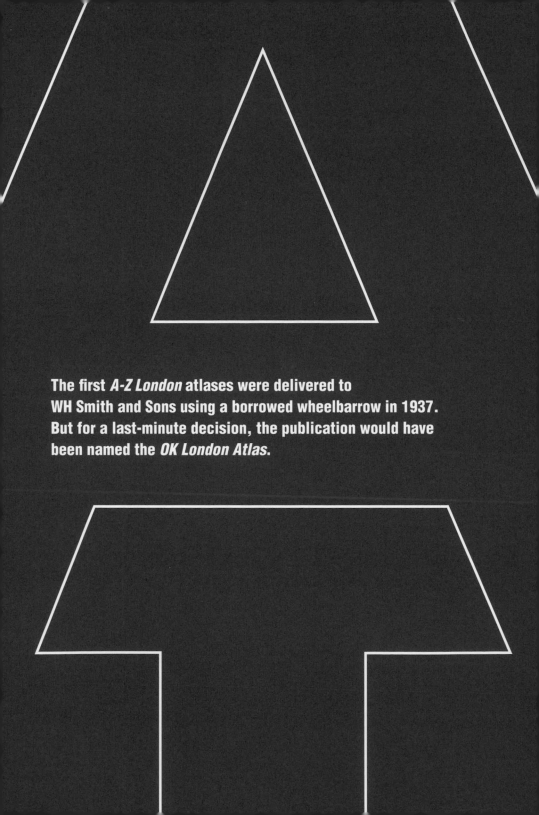

The first *A-Z London* atlases were delivered to
WH Smith and Sons using a borrowed wheelbarrow in 1937.
But for a last-minute decision, the publication would have
been named the *OK London Atlas*.

MAP 1

Buckingham Palace
London, England

The official London residence
of the British monarch

First built for the Duke of Buckingham in 1703, the palace was bought by King George III in 1761 and has seen many extensions and additions since then – most recently, the construction of the east front and balcony in the early twentieth century. The balcony and its approach along The Mall have often been a focal point for British people during times of celebration or mourning.

The first monarch to live in Buckingham Palace was Queen Victoria, and it has been the official London residence of every reigning monarch since.

The palace has 775 rooms, including 240 bedrooms and 78 bathrooms. It boasts a cinema, a swimming pool, a post office, a police station and a jewellery workshop. There are also more than 800 staff working in the palace. It is like a private village in the very centre of London.

QUESTIONS

It's on the Map

1 | Can you find a yard that shares its name with a type of firework?

2 | Can you find a feature named after an animal, that adjoins directly to another feature named after someone who cares for animals?

3 | The largest feature on the map is Green Park, but how many other locations with a colour as one of the words in their name can you find?

Cryptic Challenges

4 | Can you find a street that, spoken out loud, would sound immodest?

5 | Where might heavenly creatures go for justice?

6 | Can you locate a very consistent unit of distance?

The Knowledge

7 | Which location, built between 1825 and 1827, is the official London residence of the Prince of Wales?

8 | What was the name of the actor who played the ninth incarnation of Doctor Who? His surname can be found on the map.

9 | There is a location on the map that shares its name with a family whose barn Marty crashes into in *Back to the Future*. What is it?

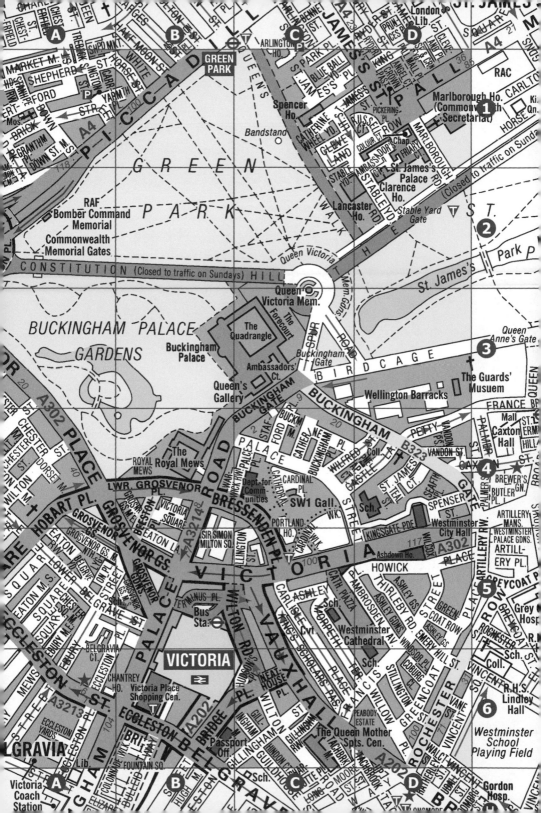

MAP 2

Tower of London
London, England

Her Majesty's Royal Palace and Fortress of the Tower of London

The Fortress of the Tower of London is a historic castle located on the north bank of the River Thames in Central London. It lies within the London Borough of Tower Hamlets, separated from the eastern edge of the square mile of the City of London by the open space known as Tower Hill.

It was founded towards the end of 1066 as part of the Norman Conquest of England. The White Tower, which gives the entire castle its name, was built by William the Conqueror in 1078 and was a resented symbol of oppression, inflicted upon London by the new ruling elite. The castle was used as a prison from 1100 (for Ranulf Flambard) until 1952 (the Kray twins) although that was not its primary purpose.

A grand palace early in its history, it served as a royal residence. As a whole, the Tower is a complex of several buildings set within two concentric rings of defensive walls and a moat. There were several phases of expansion, mainly under Kings Richard I, Henry III and Edward I in the twelfth and thirteenth centuries. The general layout established by the late thirteenth century remains, despite later activity on the site.

QUESTIONS

It's on the Map

1 | Can you find the name of a mythical creature within a map block of the river?

2 | How many complete blue bicycle symbols can you find on the map?

3 | How many different herbs and spices can you find on the map?

Cryptic Challenges

4 | Can you find a location that sounds really angry?

5 | What 60s hair-do is this map sporting?

6 | Can you find a location on the map which encompasses an entire year?

The Knowledge

7 | What 'S' is a general term for the Arabs at the time of the Crusades, and which can also be found on the map?

8 | Which 'C' is a large wading bird of the sandpiper family, with a long, downcurved beak and brown plumage? There is a street on the map which shares its name.

9 | Can you find a renowned seventeenth-century diarist's surname on the map? He was also Chief Secretary to the Admiralty under both Charles II and James II.

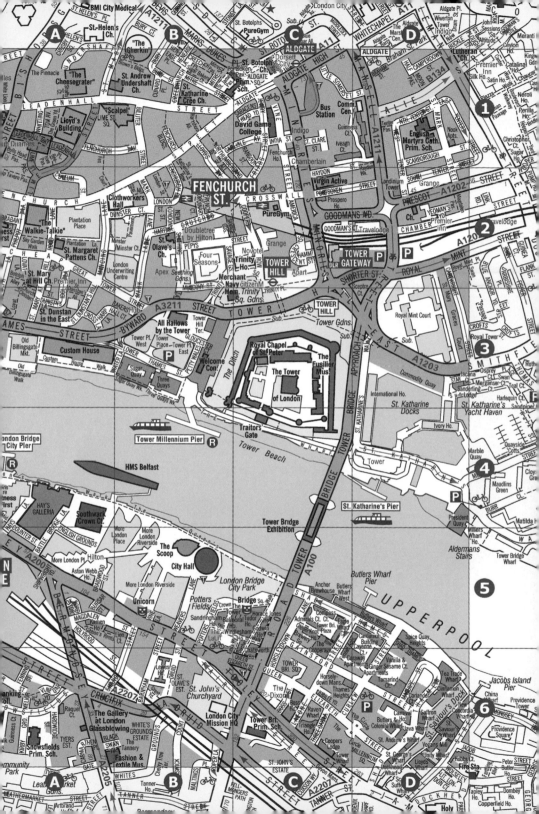

To ensure that the first *A-Z London* was as up to date as possible Phyllis Pearsall walked the streets of London each day for hours on end marking map revisions and noting house numbers.

MAP 3

Greenwich
London, England

Home to the Meridian Line

Greenwich is a Royal Borough in South East London on the banks of the River Thames. It has a long maritime history and in Greenwich Park you can find both the Prime Meridian Line from which we get Greenwich Mean Time, and also the National Maritime Museum and Royal Observatory.

Greenwich was the site of a royal palace from the fourteenth century, and both King Henry VIII and Elizabeth I were born there. The palace later became the Royal Naval College and finally a part of the University of Greenwich.

Greenwich is connected to North London by the Greenwich Foot Tunnel. The tunnel's entrance is a glass-topped rotunda next to the famous Scottish sailing ship, the *Cutty Sark*, which is also a popular tourist destination in this leafy part of London.

QUESTIONS

It's on the Map

1 | Can you find a tunnel which runs parallel with a DLR line?

2 | Can you locate three four-legged animals on the map?

3 | Where on the map might you expect to find an acrobatic performance?

Cryptic Challenges

4 | What location sounds like somewhere that a performing group might be prohibited from sitting?

5 | On which elevation might you expect to get lost?

6 | Which road on the map sounds like a particularly happy location?

The Knowledge

7 | Which Tom Hardy film, set entirely in a car, can you find on the map?

8 | Who was the longest-serving editor of the *Daily Mail* in its history, being in the role from 1992 to 2018? His surname can be found on the map.

9 | Can you find the full name of the person who was governor of Pennsylvania until the American Revolution?

MAP 4

The Oldest Terraced Houses in London, England

Historic terraced houses

On the West side of Newington Green, a small park in North London set between the fashionable areas of Islington and Hackney, is a row of terraced houses that have survived for nearly four hundred years. The small red-brick houses were built in the mid-seventeenth century when the area was still a rural village and have survived the Great Fire of London, two world wars, and the post-war redevelopment of the city.

Four stories high and each only a few metres wide, the houses have been home to interesting characters ranging from MPs to poets, and when the famous preacher and political dissident, Dr Richard Price, moved in in 1754 he was visited by many of the founding fathers of America, including Benjamin Franklin, John Adams and Thomas Jefferson. Another visitor to Newington Green some thirty years later was the early feminist and radical thinker Mary Wollstonecraft. At the time Newington was known as a hotbed of political and religious dissent and many of the key thinkers from that era are buried in nearby Abney Park Cemetery.

QUESTIONS

It's on the Map

1 | What road shares its name with a famous sunglasses brand?

2 | Can you find somewhere that sounds like a lovely street to live on?

3 | Can you locate a thoroughfare whose first word begins with an animal sound?

Cryptic Challenges

4 | Can you find an avenue on the map that sounds like it could be related to Kate and Pippa?

5 | The name of a famous castaway can be found on the map, who – if you expand the street name abbreviation – sounds like he could be crying. Where is he on the map?

6 | Which road might be familiar to unsuccessful golfers?

The Knowledge

7 | Which poet famously wandered 'lonely as a cloud'? His surname can be found on the map.

8 | Which composer, best-known for *Tubular Bells*, can you spot the surname of on the map?

9 | Which castle is the principal seat of the Howard family, whose heads are the Dukes of Norfolk? The name of the castle can be found on the map.

Colour printing was expensive, so the *A-Z London Street Atlas* was printed in black and white. This determined how road classifications were shown with both A and B roads drawn wider than minor roads. A heavier casing line on A roads was also added to help distinguish them further. A coloured edition of the *A-Z* was introduced in 1985, ultimately replacing the black and white book which was discontinued in 2001.

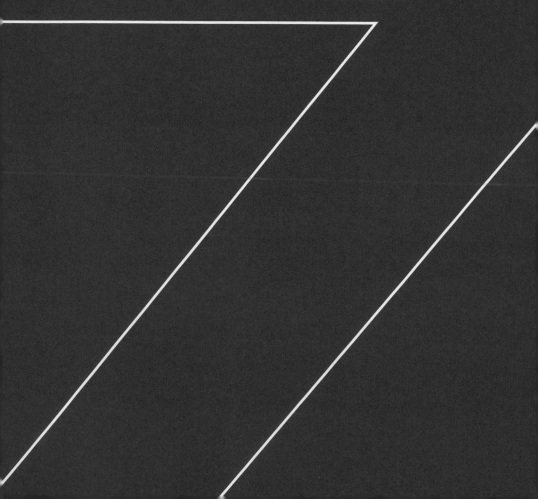

MAP 5

City of London Cemetery
London, England

The largest cemetery in the UK

Between Manor Park and Wanstead Park in East London is the City of London Cemetery. The cemetery is the largest municipal burial ground in the UK and probably in Europe, with more than a million people interred within its grounds.

The first burial took place in 1856 and, due to a shortage of space, graves are now being reused every 75 years. As well as the burials that have initially taken place in the cemetery, the grounds also contain the bodies from thirty churchyards that were destroyed during the Blitz, their bodies having been moved here after the war.

Among the more famous people buried in the City of London Cemetery are Lord Mayors of London, victims of Jack the Ripper, Winston Churchill's nanny, and World Cup winner Sir Bobby Moore.

QUESTIONS

It's on the Map

1 | Can you find two places on the map which each contain a different name for the same chess piece?

2 | How many places of worship marked with a cross can you find on the map?

3 | Can you identify a location that shares its name with a famous wizard?

Cryptic Challenges

4 | If you swap 'avenue' for 'heaven', you end up with nirvana in this location.

5 | Once you expand a street abbreviation, can you find what sounds like a warning for an approaching visitor from space?

6 | The main map feature is a cemetery, but can you find a 'grave' concealed somewhere outside the cemetery?

The Knowledge

7 | Which street on the map shares its name with the most populous of all Canadian cities?

8 | Can you find a place on the map which shares its name with the British quiz show where you might meet The Dark Destroyer?

9 | What is the largest island in the Firth of Clyde? Can you find a road that shares its name?

MAP 6

Hampton Court Palace London, England

Royal Palace

Twelve miles southwest of Central London, on the banks of the River Thames, stands Hampton Court Palace, the famous home of King Henry VIII. The palace was initially built for Cardinal Thomas Wolsey, a favourite of King Henry's. But when Wolsey refused to help annul the king's marriage he was imprisoned and the palace was given to the crown.

Henry enlarged the palace, but it was William III one hundred years later who would make the most dramatic changes to the palace, as he tried to make it rival Versailles. For this reason the palace has two distinct architectural styles, Tudor and baroque.

Set in picturesque parkland, but easily accessible from Central London, the palace has often been used as a filming location, most recently in *Sherlock Holmes*, *Pirates of the Caribbean*, and *The Favourite*.

QUESTIONS

It's on the Map

1 | How many sets of disabled toilets (marked with a red triangle containing a 'T') can you find in columns B, C and D? And how many car park symbols can you find in columns A and B?

2 | Can you find a road that is only open at certain times of the day?

3 | Can you locate a section of a single road that forms an almost perfect four-sided rectangle?

Cryptic Challenges

4 | Can you find a location that sounds as if it contains a lot of tobacco?

5 | Where might a green citrus fruit go for a stroll?

6 | This road is named after a mode of transport that could itself never use it. Which street is this referring to?

The Knowledge

7 | King Henry VIII's first wife took her name from Castile, in which Spanish region? Can you find a street on the map that contains the answer?

8 | Which 2005 film by director Michael Bay stars Ewan McGregor and Scarlett Johansson? Its full name can be found on the map.

9 | Which eponymous scientific law specifies how the pressure of a gas tends to increase as the volume of a container decreases? Which street on the map contains its discoverer's name?

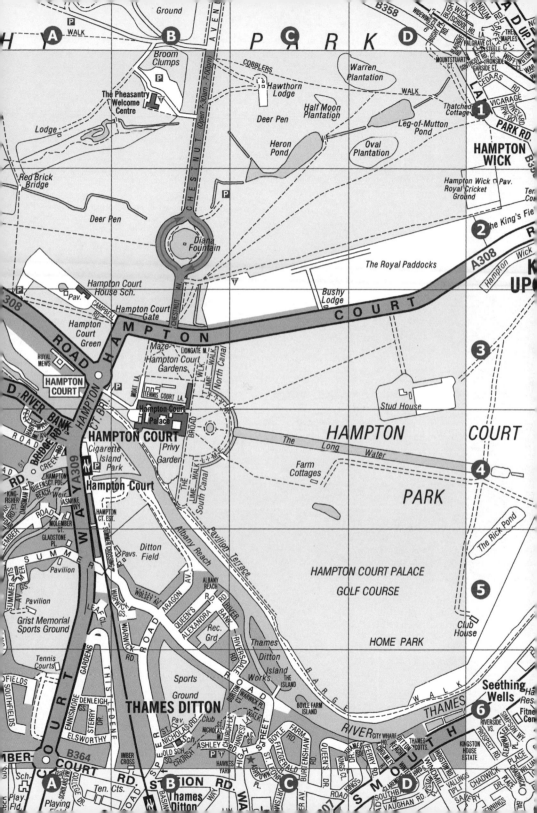

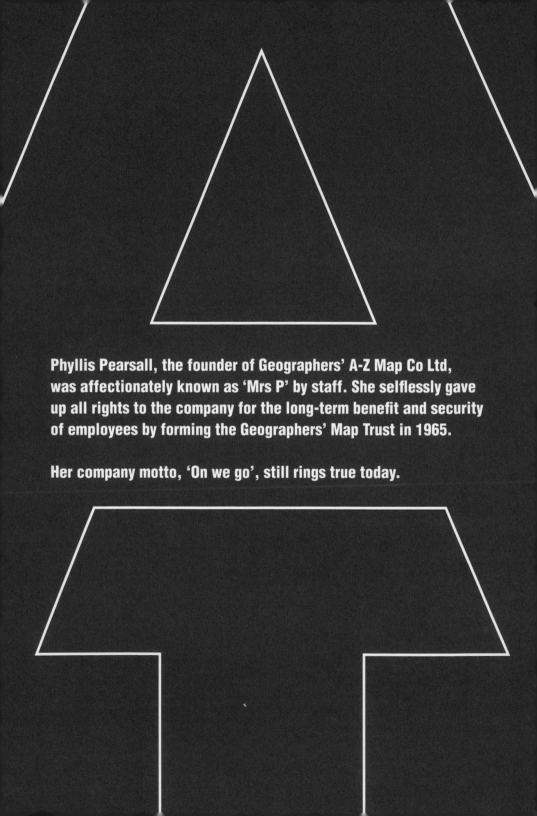

Phyllis Pearsall, the founder of Geographers' A-Z Map Co Ltd, was affectionately known as 'Mrs P' by staff. She selflessly gave up all rights to the company for the long-term benefit and security of employees by forming the Geographers' Map Trust in 1965.

Her company motto, 'On we go', still rings true today.

MAP 7

Hastings
East Sussex, England

Town linked to the Battle of Hastings

A fishing town on the coast of South East England, Hastings is forever associated with the battle of 1066 in which William the Conqueror defeated the last Saxon king, Harold Godwinson. The battle marked the beginning of the Norman Conquest, and shaped much of British identity and language in the millennium to come.

The town today is notable for its ruined castle, and its lack of a natural harbour – its fleet of fishing boats must launch from the beach. Usually a sleepy place, Hastings comes alive at the start of May each year when both the Jack-in-the-Green and Maydayrun festivals see thousands of motorcyclists and partygoers fill the streets. Hastings is also famous as the world record holder for gathering the most pirates together in one place each November on Hastings Pirate Day.

QUESTIONS

It's on the Map

1 | Can you find an oval-shaped street with an ironically angular name?

2 | There are two separate tourist attractions that share an intrepid-sounding word. What is it?

3 | How many educational establishments can you find marked on the map?

Cryptic Challenges

4 | Can you find a board game utility that is synonymous with crying?

5 | Where does it sound like long-handled brushes grow?

6 | Can you locate a street that is heard to be strongly and solidly built?

The Knowledge

7 | In film, what name has been followed by 'identity', 'supremacy', 'ultimatum' and 'legacy'? It has even been preceded by a name. Can you find it on the map?

8 | Which actor won an Oscar in 2015 for his performance in *The Theory of Everything*? His surname can be found on the map.

9 | Which country sent Viking raiders to Britain under the rule of Sweyn Forkbeard in 1013? Where on the map does it appear?

MAP 8

Cambridge City Centre England

Home to the University of Cambridge

The University of Cambridge was founded in 1209 and ever since then has been the main focus of this small city in the East of England. Just fifty miles from London, it is famous for its quiet quadrangles, gothic buildings and the River Cam which flows through the centre of town. The city sits on the edge of the Fens, a large expanse of wetland, and is in most places just a few metres above sea level.

Though significant parts of the city are dedicated to tourism, technological industries and the world-class Addenbrooke's Hospital, the economic focus of Cambridge is its many colleges and University Library, one of the largest legal deposit libraries in the world. The University of Cambridge has more Nobel Prize-winners than any other institution in the world, and was also the site of the world's first game of association football in 1848.

QUESTIONS

It's on the Map

1 | How many red bicycles, labelling cycle paths, can you find?

2 | There are various places of worship marked on the map, but in which map square would you find the Round Church?

3 | Can you find a street with a flower for a name?

Cryptic Challenges

4 | There are various religiously connected names on the map, but can you find a place that sounds like it contains holy fragments?

5 | Can you find an inn in the attic of a building?

6 | If this was London, where might speakers congregate?

The Knowledge

7 | Can you find a landmark that takes its name from a famous crossing in Venice?

8 | Which country joined the European Union on the same day as Spain? Can you find it on the map?

9 | On what street have Peter, Nelson, Peta, Sybil, Freya, Larry and Munich Mouser all lived? Its namesake can be located on the map.

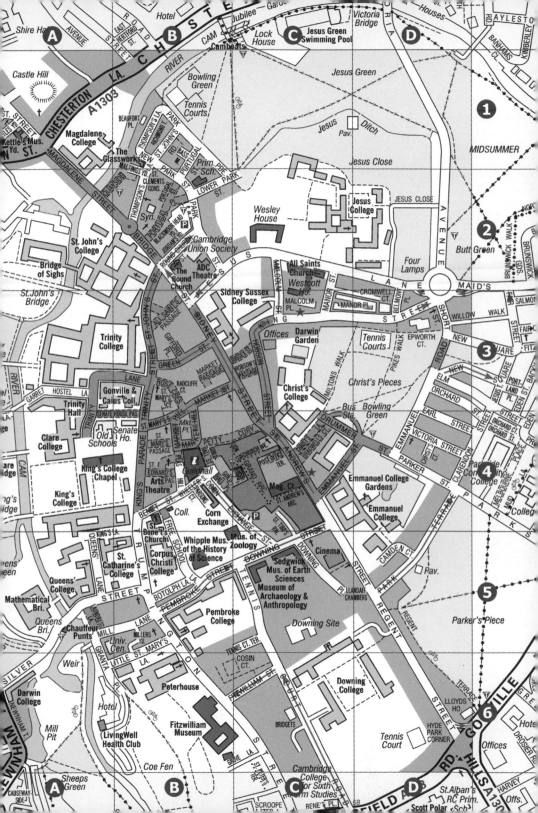

Phyllis Pearsall's family nickname was Pig – the initials of her name: Phyllis Isobella Gross.

MAP 9

Caerphilly Castle
Caerphilly, Wales

13th century castle

At the end of the Rhymney Valley in South Wales, the town of Caerphilly is famous for three things: its castle, its cheese and Tommy Cooper.

The castle was built in the thirteenth century as the English nobles sought to conquer Wales. It is a concentric castle surrounded by a complicated array of artificial lakes making up one of the most elaborate water defences in Britain. Its dams are also fortified and there are further defensive islands in the lakes. It is the largest castle in Wales and the second largest in the UK, after Windsor. Caerphilly Castle probably last served a military purpose in the Glyndŵr Rising of the fifteenth century.

Caerphilly cheese was a more recent invention however, developed in the Industrial Revolution as a food that could provide moisture and a high salt content for the coal miners of the surrounding valleys. One such coal miner was the father of Tommy Cooper the legendary comedian and magician who was born in Caerphilly, where a statue of him still stands.

QUESTIONS

It's on the Map

1 | Can you find three 'Warren's, each in a different size of writing?

2 | There is a cluster of buildings whose outlines appear to be attempting to spell 'FOB'. Can you locate them?

3 | Can you identify a word on the map that fits the pattern '?w?w?w?', where each '?' is a letter? None of the letters are vowels.

Cryptic Challenges

4 | Which location sounds like the heaviest weight on the map?

5 | Which street is good at catching and cornering?

6 | Can you find somewhere that goods vehicles are grown?

The Knowledge

7 | Which former CIA employee released classified documents in 2013 that revealed the extent of various government-run global surveillance programmes? His name can be found on the map.

8 | Which Welsh entertainer was famous for his red fez? He has a statue in Caerphilly, which is marked on the map.

9 | Which ruler, who can be found on the map, was known as the 'Hammer of the Scots'?

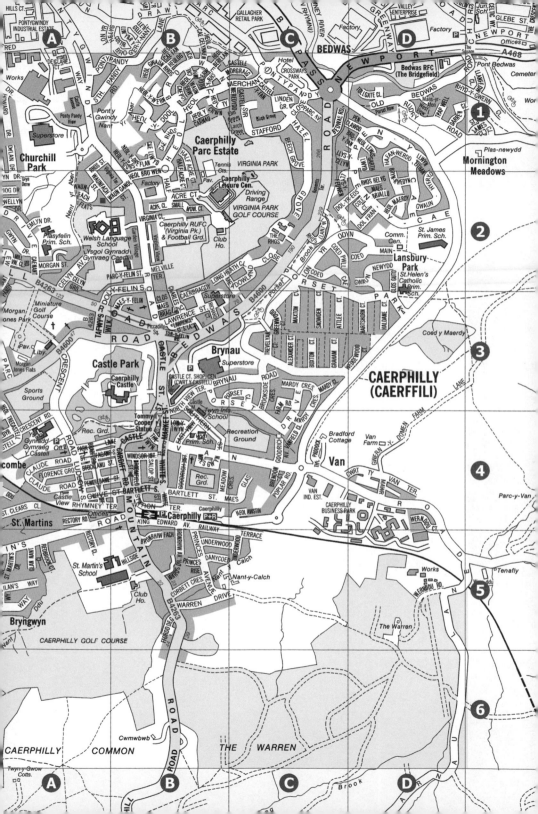

MAP 10

Edinburgh Castle
Edinburgh, Scotland

Historic castle

On a prominent volcanic rock, at the head of The Royal Mile, and overlooking the old and new towns of Scotland's capital, sits Edinburgh Castle. There has been a royal fortress on the rock since the time of King David in the twelfth century and there is evidence of human habitation here a millennium before that.

In the castle's 1,100-year history it has seen twenty-six sieges, making it one of the most attacked castles in the world. The most famous perhaps were during the Scottish Wars of Independence in the fourteenth century and the most recent was during the Jacobite Rising of 1745.

Each year in August, the castle's esplanade plays host to the Royal Military Tattoo, when more than 200,000 visitors watch a display of marching, music, flyovers and fireworks organised by the British military. At the same time the International Festival and Festival Fringe transform Edinburgh into the largest arts festival in the world and dramatically increase the city's population while they are on.

QUESTIONS

It's on the Map

1 | How many post offices (indicated with a red star) are marked on the map?

2 | Where would blooms be able to help you tell the time?

3 | Can you find a building that is a cross in both name and appearance?

Cryptic Challenges

4 | If a yellow-coloured family from Springfield lent you money, it would be a... what?

5 | In what place might a cryptic question most appropriately be set?

6 | Can you change a double letter to a single letter in order to reveal a fantasy monster on the map?

The Knowledge

7 | The woman often considered to be the founder of modern nursing shares her surname with which street?

8 | Which name is shared between separate leading companies that manufacture tyres in one case, and sports equipment in the other? Can you find it on the map?

9 | What blend of tea is thought to have been named after a British prime minister who served from 1830 to 1834? His name appears on the map.

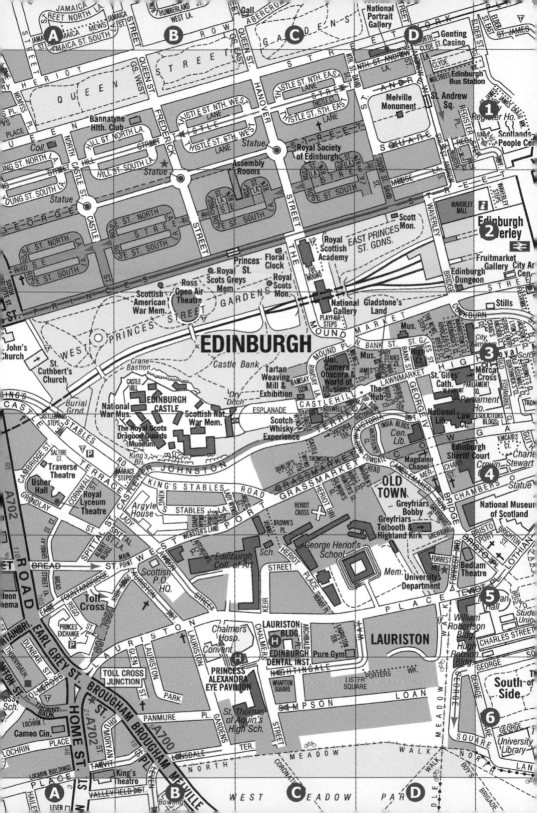

SPORT

The first maps were drawn entirely by hand, including the naming of streets and towns. Draughtsmen were expected to draw and letter 18–20 streets per hour. In 1938 it would have taken a draughtsman approximately twelve weeks to create a finished publication.

MAP 11

Wembley
London, England

Renowned arena and stadium

Synonymous with its arena and stadium, Wembley is an area of North West London that has hosted some of the most significant cultural and sporting events of the last century. Originally a manufacturing suburb of London in which metals, power tools and scientific equipment were produced, it has been largely redeveloped with a focus on sport and leisure.

The first major venue to be built in Wembley was the National Stadium in 1923. Many other venues and features were constructed in Wembley Park for the Empire Exhibition of 1924–25 which saw taster-sized exhibits from all of Britain's fifty-eight colonies – excluding the Irish Free State and Gambia.

In 1948 Wembley Park and Stadium played host to the Olympics in a post-war celebration of Britain's survival. Today, Wembley is dominated by the great arch of the New Wembley Stadium which was constructed in 2007 and was a host venue for the 2012 Olympic Games. It is still England's national stadium, playing host to the FA Cup and League Cup finals each year.

QUESTIONS

It's on the Map

1 | Can you find a street that shares its name with the age at which life is sometimes said to begin?

2 | Can you spot the heroine of *The Wizard of Oz* on the map?

3 | There is a word that refers to a magical lucky charm on the map. What is it?

Cryptic Challenges

4 | Where might you find an elevated farm building?

5 | What could be a point of 157.5 degrees?

6 | Where could you find what sounds like angry routes?

The Knowledge

7 | Which poet, also known for her semi-autobiographical novel *The Bell Jar*, died at the age of 30 in 1963? Her first name can be found on the map.

8 | Which Hampshire town hosts the world's second largest air show? An abbreviated version of its name can be found on the map.

9 | Which road has the same name as an Italian-designed tilting train used in many European countries?

MAP 12

Queen Elizabeth Olympic Park London, England

Sports development for the Olympic Games

Renamed after her Diamond Jubilee, Queen Elizabeth Olympic Park in Stratford, East London is a huge sports and leisure development that covers a former brownfield site as well as part of Hackney Marshes.

Built for the 2012 Olympic Games, the event was a huge success though there were many criticisms of the park itself including controversy over its destruction of a green site, and the many extravagant and unusual architectural features that dominate it. The most prominent of these is the ArcelorMittal Orbit tower, a roller-coaster-like observation tower and sculpture which is Britain's largest piece of public art.

The park has a post-Olympic life, and its swimming pools, tennis courts, theatre and velodrome are now open to the public, while the Olympic Stadium now plays host to West Ham United FC.

QUESTIONS

It's on the Map

1 | Can you find a street that shares its name with a season?

2 | Which street has a name that is an appropriate description for birthdays, anniversaries or New Year's Eve?

3 | Which DLR station sounds like somewhere you'd make a dessert?

Cryptic Challenges

4 | Where should 'Sirs' cross the river?

5 | It's where you should place your rubbish, perhaps – especially if you're feeling lucky.

6 | If shop employees can't reach all of the shelves, the store needs something that sounds like this.

The Knowledge

7 | Why was the London Stadium built, and what was it previously known as?

8 | What road shares its name with a musical brother-sister duo that were active during the Seventies?

9 | What prolific English film director was responsible for *Rebecca*, *North by Northwest* and *Rear Window*? Can you find a street that shares his last name?

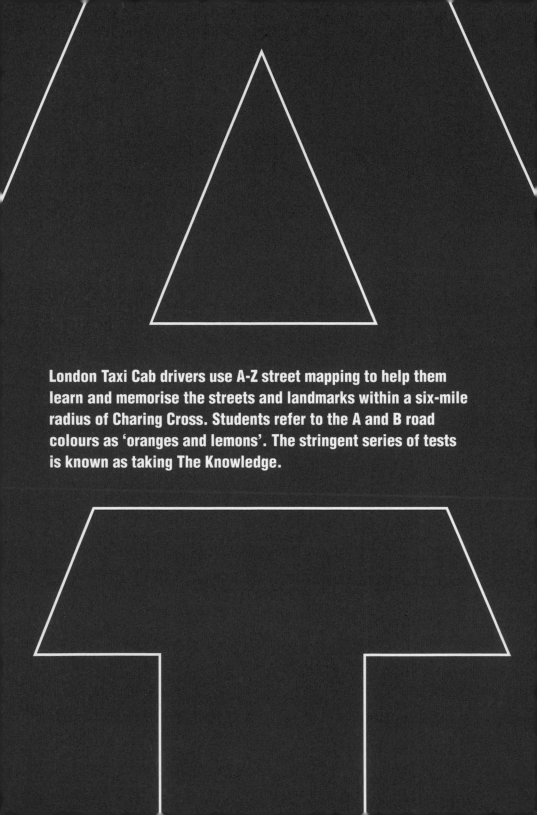

London Taxi Cab drivers use A-Z street mapping to help them learn and memorise the streets and landmarks within a six-mile radius of Charing Cross. Students refer to the A and B road colours as 'oranges and lemons'. The stringent series of tests is known as taking The Knowledge.

MAP 13

Wimbledon
London, England
The UK's tennis hub

Absorbed into London in 1965, Wimbledon is a large
neighbourhood of South West London some seven miles
from the city centre. It is famous as the home of lawn
tennis, and each year it hosts the Wimbledon Tennis
Championship, the oldest and most prestigious tennis
contest in the world. It is well-known for its strict dress
code, its royal patronage, and the strawberries and cream
that are traditionally eaten at matches. In 2017 spectators
consumed 34,000 kg of strawberries and more than 10,000
litres of cream.

In 2018 the Lawn Tennis Association purchased the
neighbouring Wimbledon Golf Club and they hope to
expand the tournament over its grounds to provide a better
visitor experience. As well as tennis and golf, cricket and
croquet are played on the site.

QUESTIONS

It's on the Map

1 | Centre Court is a famous feature of the All England Club, but it is written elsewhere on the map. Can you find it, and work out why?

2 | Can you find a street that sounds like somewhere milk products would perambulate?

3 | There is a building in the shape of a 'J' on the map. Can you locate it?

Cryptic Challenges

4 | Can you find somewhere that sounds like an appropriate place to do chilly origami?

5 | What should you mind, according to the London Underground?

6 | If you wished you had better vision, you would like to be able to do something that sounds like this.

The Knowledge

7 | Murray Road can be found in A6, but when Andy Murray won the Gentlemen's Singles at Wimbledon in 2013 how long had it been since a British player had won that title?

8 | What animated adult show, which first aired in 1997 and has broadcast more than twenty seasons, did Trey Parker and Matt Stone create? Its name can be found on the map.

9 | What ancient Roman emperor's name replaced the month that was formally named 'Sextilis'? Find a road on the map that bears his name.

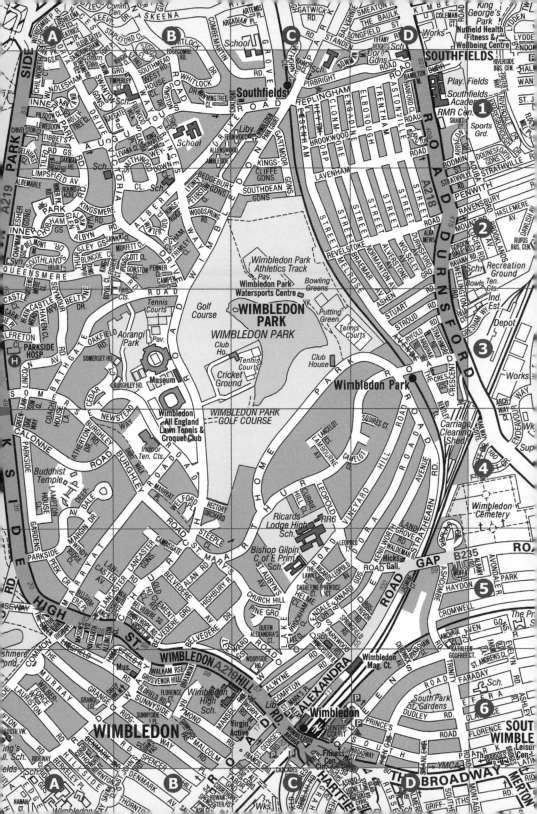

MAP 14

The Oval
London, England

Cricket ground

The earliest recorded first class cricket match played on Kennington Common in the South London borough of Lambeth was between London and Dartford in 1724. The Common was enclosed in the early 1800s by the Royal Family, and by 1840 it was a market garden owned by the Duchy of Cornwall. But cricket returned in 1845 when the land was leased to Surrey County Cricket Club and The Oval was built.

Considered one of the spiritual homes of English cricket, The Oval hosts the last English test match of each season and regularly features other international games. In 1868 it hosted England vs Australia as part of the first ever cricket tour by a foreign side and in 1889 it became the first artificially lit sports arena in the world when gas lamps were installed.

During the Second World War The Oval was requisitioned by the government and used as a prisoner of war camp.

QUESTIONS

It's on the Map

1 | How many street names that end in 'Mews' can you find on the map? This is often abbreviated to 'M.'

2 | Can you find a street that shares a name with one of the two main land masses that make up New Zealand?

3 | The name of a meat knife can be found on the map. Where?

Cryptic Challenges

4 | The letters 'N U S _ M E V M' form a well-known sequence. Can you work out which letter is missing, and then find the corresponding word on the map?

5 | Can you find a boring-sounding building?

6 | If some grain-crushers had an argument, it would be a… what?

The Knowledge

7 | What 2007 film about teenage pregnancy stars Ellen Page and Michael Cera? Can you find its title on the map?

8 | The Oval (B3) is one of the world's most famous cricket grounds – but what is the distance between the wickets on a cricket pitch?

9 | Pencil leads are not actually made of lead, but rather which material that can be found on the map?

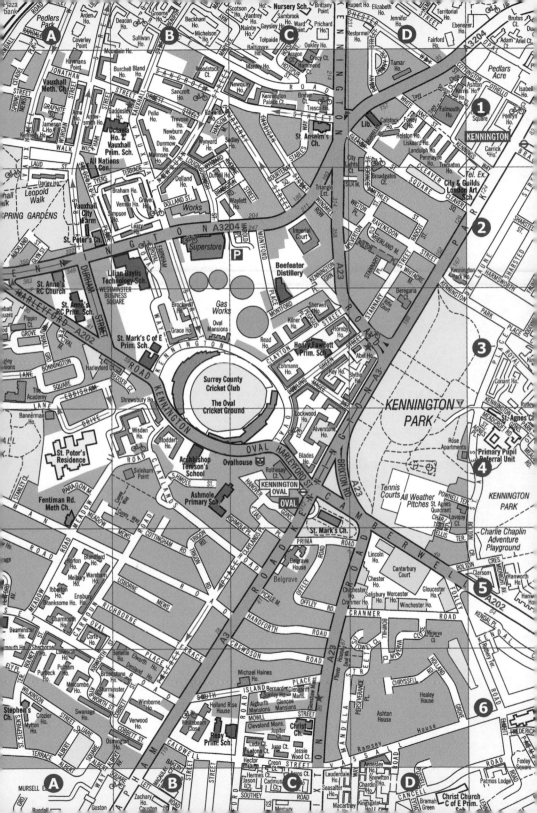

Today's joined A–Z logo was designed by newspaper cartoonist Roy Dewar in 1972. The company incorporated 'A–Z' into its registered name the following year.

MAP 15

Cheltenham Racecourse Prestbury Park near Cheltenham, England

Horse racing arena

On the edge of the Cotswolds in rural Gloucestershire, South West England, Cheltenham Racecourse is a horse racing arena that hosts the prestigious annual Gold Cup. The racecourse has capacity for 67,500 spectators and The Centaur, an auditorium on the site, has space for a further 4,000 standing audience members for concerts.

Made up of the old and new courses, Cheltenham has hosted flat races since 1818 and it still has its own working steam railway station, though it is not connected to the national rail network.

As well as races, the site has hosted Wychwood and Greenbelt music festivals and is the site for graduations from the University of Gloucester.

QUESTIONS

It's on the Map

1 | How many roundabouts can you find on the map? Don't include circular roads which have their name labelled on them in your count.

2 | Can you find a building in the shape of a letter 'H'?

3 | There are two types of nut on the map. Can you find them both? One is in the plural.

Cryptic Challenges

4 | Can you find what sounds like a pool slide?

5 | Which is the nicer of any pair of residences on the map?

6 | Locate a multi-pointed place of justice.

The Knowledge

7 | What was the name of Myanmar prior to 1989? Can you find it on the map?

8 | Which French battle of the First World War lasted for five months and stretched along a fifty-mile front? It resulted in the greatest loss of Britons in a single day in history. Can you find a street that shares its name with the river that the battle is named after?

9 | Which is the second-most expensive location in Monopoly? A road of the same name can be found on the map.

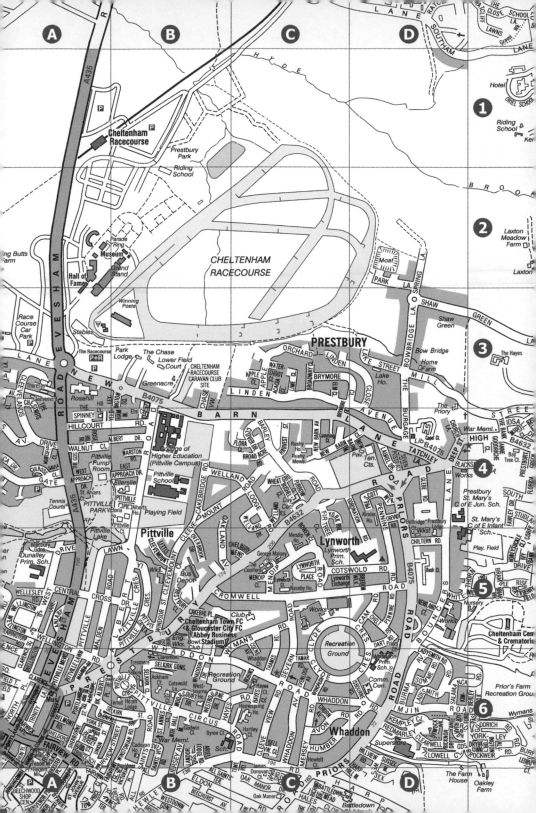

MAP 16

Rugby
Warwickshire, England

Birthplace of rugby

On the banks of the River Avon, the English town of Rugby in Warwickshire gave its name to the sport when a schoolboy, William Webb Ellis, picked up a football and ran with it. He is still commemorated at Rugby School where that first game took place.

The town itself has existed since Iron Age times and was mentioned in the Domesday Book. Rugby School was founded in 1567, by which time Rugby was a bustling market town. In fact, the school was founded by Queen Elizabeth I's grocer. Growth was slow until the arrival of the railway and motorway made Rugby a significant transport interchange in the nineteenth and twentieth centuries.

As well as rugby and railways, the town is also famous as the birthplace of the jet engine. Frank Whittle built the world's first prototype jet engine at the British Thomson-Houston works in 1937 and revolutionised air travel.

QUESTIONS

It's on the Map

1 | Can you find a building in the shape of a letter 'E'?

2 | What map marking, at least on this map, is unique to the war memorial?

3 | Can you find two adjacent buildings on the map that, along with the space between them, form what looks like the French flag?

Cryptic Challenges

4 | Can you find New York City?

5 | Where is entertainment pulverized?

6 | Which two streets represent the start of the yearly Boat Race?

The Knowledge

7 | According to the nursery rhyme, where does the Muffin Man reside? Can you locate its namesake on the map?

8 | Which Scottish inventor is credited with the invention of the telephone? Find a road on the map that uses his surname.

9 | Where, on the map, is the legendary origin of the modern sport of rugby?

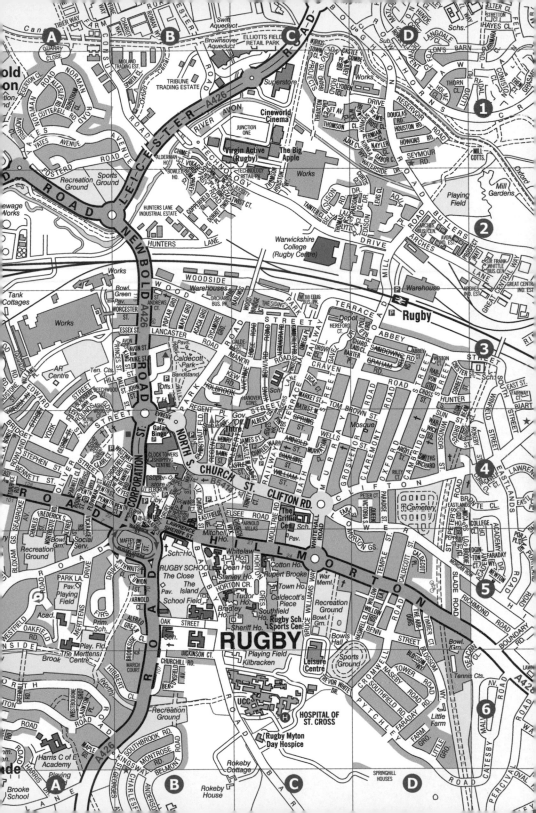

Map restrictions were put in place by the government for the duration of the Second World War, which included the removal of detailed street maps from sale. During this time the company switched to producing war maps for newspapers.

MAP 17

Loughborough University
Loughborough, England

Prestigious sports campus

In the town of Loughborough, Leicestershire, in England's East Midlands, Loughborough University is a modern university that first emerged as Loughborough Technical Institute in 1909 and was awarded university status in 1966. Since 2015 it has also operated a second campus at the Olympic Park in London. But its roots are in Leicestershire and in practical teaching and research.

Sites of interest around the campus include its walled garden, the 'garden of remembrance', the Hazlerigg-Rutland Hall fountain-courtyard, a nine hole golf course and the Bastard Gates, but they aren't an insult, they were named after William Bastard. The university also has a series of beehives and produces its own honey.

QUESTIONS

It's on the Map

1 | There is a road on the map that is named after a place where horses are often kept. What is it?

2 | Can you find the name of a type of hat on the map?

3 | Can you find a road that shares its name with a place where someone would live in seclusion?

Cryptic Challenges

4 | Where on the map could represent the culmination of a young child's pre-school?

5 | Can you find somewhere to escape to?

6 | When you pot a pool ball, where does it end up?

The Knowledge

7 | Which British athlete, and graduate of Loughborough University, posted new world records in the 800 metres, 1500 metres and the mile within the space of forty-one days in 1979? Can you find his surname on the map?

8 | Which British adventurer, born in 1901, became the first person to sail single-handedly around the world in 1967 aboard his yacht *Gipsy Moth IV*? A road on the map shares his surname.

9 | Which athlete, whose name can be found on the map, is a three-time winner of both the London Marathon and the New York Marathon?

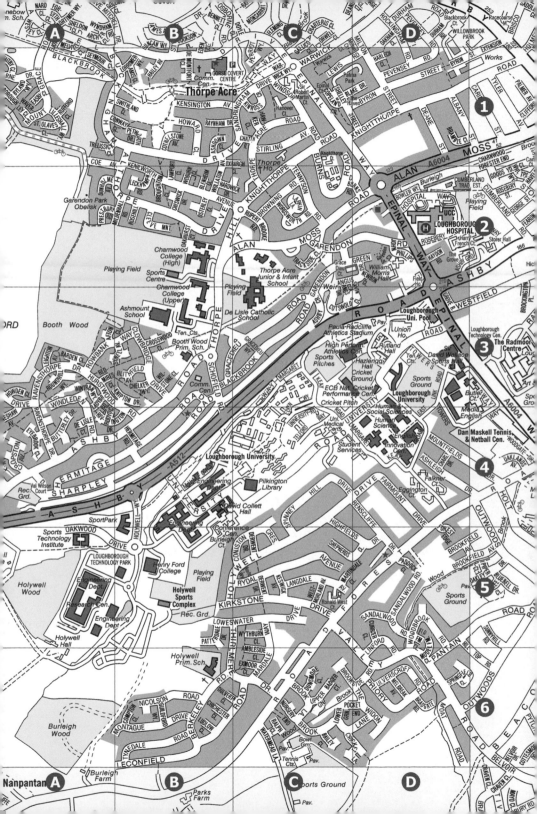

MAP 18

Cardiff Arms Park
Cardiff, Wales

Major sports arena

Cardiff Arms Park on the River Taff in Cardiff is a sports arena that has been used for rugby, cricket, boxing and bowling since the early nineteenth century. Overshadowed by its much larger neighbour The Millennium Stadium, now The Principality Stadium, Cardiff Arms Park has nevertheless hosted major sporting events including the Rugby World Cup and the Commonwealth Games since its construction in 1880.

Cardiff Arms Park is in the centre of Cardiff, close to the castle and the train station. The park's location on the banks of the River Taff was made possible by a diversion of the river by the engineer Isambard Kingdom Brunel. But its location has not always been ideal, and in 1960 it was flooded by more than 1.2 metres (4 feet) of water.

The park has also seen concerts from international stars, from Tina Turner to the Rolling Stones.

QUESTIONS

It's on the Map

1 | The three theological virtues are faith, hope and charity. Can you find one of these on the map? And can you find love, too?

2 | Can you find a road on the map that shares its name with a notable score for a cricketer?

3 | If you're being held to blame due to your responsibilities, you are in the… what? Can you find this on the map?

Cryptic Challenges

4 | Can you split a word on the map to form a useful place for a pub landlord to stock drinks?

5 | If you enjoyed a John Wayne film, you might have seen a… what?

6 | Can you find a backwards yard?

The Knowledge

7 | Which comedian, who guest-starred in *Friends*, is part of a noted female duo whose TV sketch show started on British television in 1987, with its most recent episode first airing in 2007? Can you identify the location that shares her surname?

8 | Which South Wales town is the birthplace of the founder of the National Health Service? Can you pinpoint a location on the map that shares its name?

9 | Which Welsh and British Lions fly-half, born in 1930, captained Wales and played for his country twenty-nine times in the 1950s? He was later a noted sports presenter and commentator. Can you find his surname on the map?

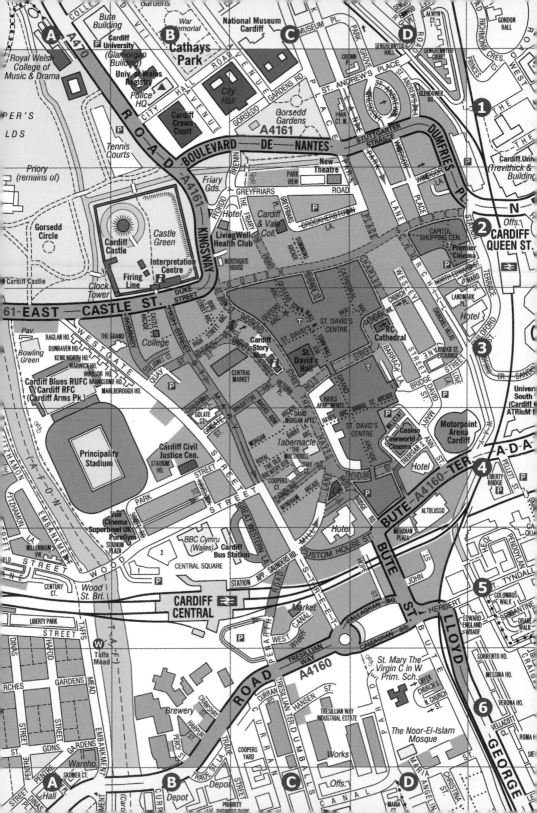

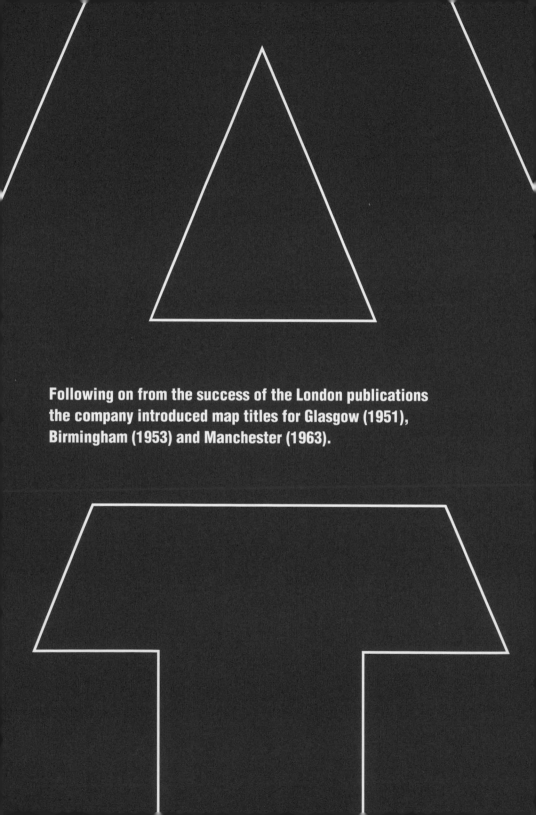

Following on from the success of the London publications the company introduced map titles for Glasgow (1951), Birmingham (1953) and Manchester (1963).

MAP 19

Celtic Park/Sir Chris Hoy Velodrome Glasgow, Scotland

Prominent Scottish stadium
and velodrome

Commonly known as Parkhead, or Paradise, Celtic Park is the second largest stadium in Scotland. It stands in the East End of the city of Glasgow and has a strong association with the working class areas of the city populated by descendants of Irish immigrants. As well as hosting major European football games for Celtic, the park has played host to international games for Scotland and the opening ceremony of the Commonwealth Games. Its record capacity was 85,000.

The site surrounding the stadium used to be the home of Parkhead Forge, a metal works factory that employed 20,000 workers. It closed in 1976 and the area is now home to a shopping centre and sporting facilities including the Emirates Arena and the Sir Chris Hoy Velodrome named after the famous Scottish Olympian. The redevelopment took place for the Glasgow 2014 Commonwealth Games when the area saw the construction of swimming pools, the velodrome, arena and athletes' village. However, there was controversy over the clearing of established communities and destruction of Victorian housing.

QUESTIONS

It's on the Map

1 | Can you find the name of a Shakespeare play on the map?

2 | The name of a northern sea that adjoins several European countries can be found on the map. What is it?

3 | Can you identify a location that shares its name with a former long-running British TV soap opera set in Liverpool? Its final episode aired in 2003.

Cryptic Challenges

4 | Where on the map sounds like a suitable location for a sacred spring?

5 | Can you identify a place on the map that sounds like a treat for a fast-food fan?

6 | Where on the map sounds as if it could be a disappointment for someone who has cooked food for guests?

The Knowledge

7 | Which British actor, who first earned an Oscar nomination in 1999 for a film in which he starred with Matt Damon, took on the lead role in 2016 in the TV series *The Young Pope*? Can you find the location that shares his surname?

8 | Which cat, created by Jim Davis, made his first appearance in a cartoon strip in 1978 and is noted for his love of lasagne? His name can be found on the map.

9 | Which golf course in Scotland has hosted the British Open on several occasions, including in 2016? Can you identify the feature on the map that shares part of its full name?

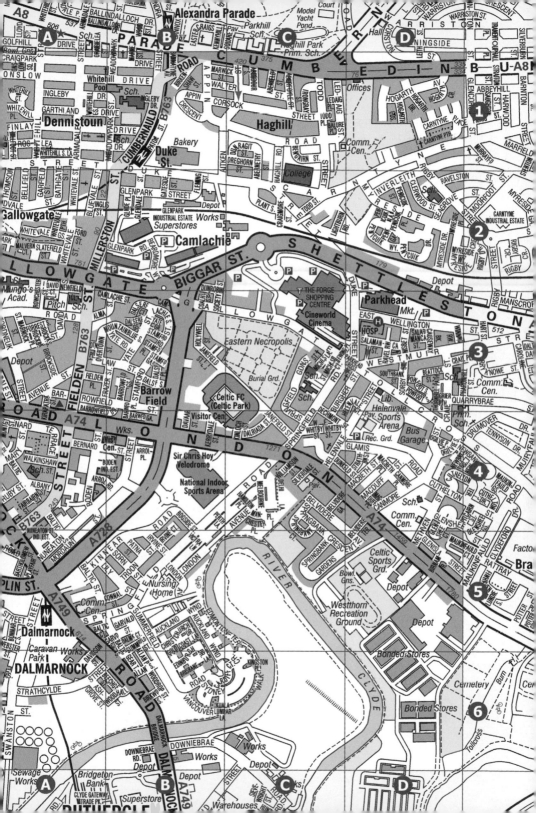

MAP 20

St Andrews
Fife, Scotland

Historic golf town

On the east coast of the Kingdom of Fife in Scotland, thirty miles northeast of Edinburgh, St Andrews is a historic university town. The name was given to the town when the claim was made that it was the resting place of the bones of the apostle St Andrew.

St Andrews is home to a ruined abbey and castle, and the third oldest English-speaking university in the world. But it is perhaps most famous as the home of golf. There are records of golf being played in the town from medieval times, and the Old Course is perhaps the most revered course in the world. The practice of having eighteen holes in a game of golf comes from this course.

There are seven courses in total at St Andrews, but winning on the Old Course is the aim for many players, with past winners including Tiger Woods and Jack Nicklaus who said, 'If a golfer is going to be remembered, he needs to win at St Andrews.'

QUESTIONS

It's on the Map

1 | Which map square contains the greatest number of car parks?

2 | Can you find the hospital (blue circle with an 'H'), police station (blue triangle) and fire station (red square)?

3 | How many churches can you find marked with a cross on the map?

Cryptic Challenges

4 | Can you find groups of twenty?

5 | A wild cat is loose on the map... or something that sounds like one, anyway. Where?

6 | Can you locate a slow and dignified street?

The Knowledge

7 | Which Broadway musical about one of the American Founding Fathers debuted in 2015? Can you find a road on the map that shares its name?

8 | What is the national flower of Scotland? It shares its name with a road on the map.

9 | Which golfer won the Masters in both 1977 and again in 1981? His surname can be found on the map.

ENTERTAINMENT

The first tunnel-boring machine (TBM) to start digging as part of London's Crossrail project was named Phyllis after our founder Phyllis Pearsall. Launched from Royal Oak in May 2012 the Phyllis TBM completed the 4.2-mile journey to Farringdon in October 2013.

MAP 21

Oxford Street
London, England

Shopping street

Undoubtedly the most famous shopping street in Europe, Oxford Street runs across the West End of London from Tottenham Court Road to Marble Arch. It has more than 300 shops and receives half a million visitors every day.

The road began as part of the Via Trinobantina, built during the Roman occupation of England, and was known as Tyburn Road in the Middle Ages when it was a site of public hangings. By the nineteenth century the road was already a well-to-do shopping area and in the early twentieth century it saw the opening of the first department stores in England. House of Fraser, John Lewis, Debenhams, and Selfridges have all had flagship stores along the street.

But Oxford Street has a darker side; it is well known for its pickpockets, and a study by King's College showed that it had the highest concentration of nitrogen dioxide pollution in the world.

QUESTIONS

It's on the Map

1 | Can you find a word on the map that refers to a small stream?

2 | There is a street that shares its name with a traditional woodworker. Can you find it? It is split over two lines, however, which makes it trickier to locate.

3 | Can you find a road on the map that shares its name (written around a curve) with part of a bicycle?

Cryptic Challenges

4 | Where might you find the Magi?

5 | Can you find somewhere very 'deer' near Bond Street?

6 | Which word on the map sounds appropriate for someone wanting to expand their toupee collection?

The Knowledge

7 | Britain's first escalator was installed at Harrod's department store in 1878, but which department store on Oxford Street (not marked on the map) was the first in the UK to offer escalators serving every floor?

8 | British sitcom actor, David White, was knighted in 2005, but by what surname is he better known? Can you find a road that shares this name?

9 | Which Oscar-winning British actor, whose surname can be found on the map, is noted for his roles in *Moulin Rouge*, two of the Harry Potter films, and three Bridget Jones films?

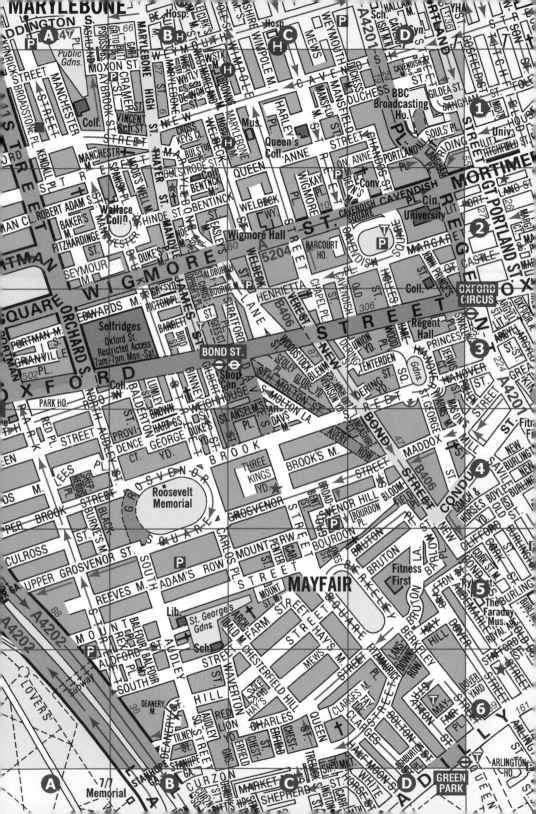

MAP 22

O$_2$ Arena
London, England

Concert venue

Built as the Millennium Dome and originally designed to host an array of exhibitions, games and experiences meant to highlight Britain's past and future, the Millennium Dome was a political failure and attracted less than half of the twelve million visitors that were projected when it opened in 2000. Its second life as London's premiere concert venue has however been a huge success.

Original proposals for the redevelopment of the dome included the building of an 'indoor city' with streets, parks and buildings within the dome. But instead it reopened in 2007 as a 20,000-capacity venue, although the arena complex actually only takes up 40 per cent of the space under the dome. The O$_2$'s roof had to be constructed on the ground and lifted, as it was impossible to use cranes inside the structure. Today the O$_2$ arena is the busiest concert venue in the world, selling more than 1.4 million tickets annually, despite being open for only 200 days a year.

QUESTIONS

It's on the Map

1 | Can you find a thoroughfare on the map that shares its name with something that serves to nudge one's memory?

2 | The capital of a mainland western European country can be found on the map. Which one?

3 | Can you locate a road on the map that shares its name with a navigational instrument, also used in surveying?

Cryptic Challenges

4 | Can you find a location on the map where you might expect to hear of an archer?

5 | This street sounds like somewhere you might go to locate a trumpet.

6 | Can you locate what might be a very proper flower?

The Knowledge

7 | Which British cyclist, who has won six Olympic gold medals, was born in Edinburgh in 1976? Can you find a road on the map that shares his surname?

8 | Which Dutch master, who died in 1669, painted *The Night Watch*? Can you find his name on the map (split over two lines)?

9 | Which band (not marked on the map) was the first to perform at The O_2 arena?

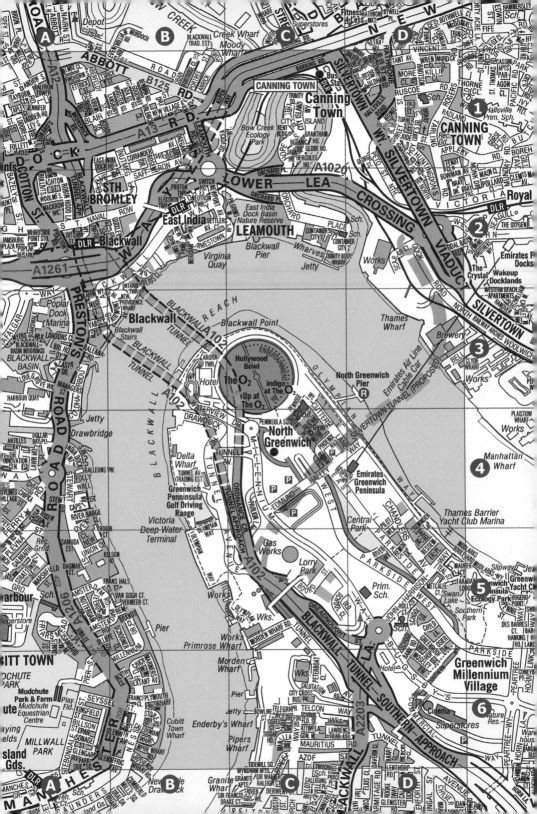

A *Coming and Going Road Atlas* was published in 1993 as a solution for map users who preferred to turn their maps around to match their direction of travel. The book had a section of traditional north-up map pages and a second section of south-up map pages. This approach may have been misguided as the atlas was not deemed successful enough to warrant a second edition.

MAP 23

London's West End
England

Tourist and theatre region
of Central London

Covering parts of the boroughs of Westminster and
Camden, London's West End is synonymous with theatre
and wealth. There are few places in Britain more expensive
to live than the West End and it is Britain's main commercial
and entertainment district. Famous for its beautiful Victorian
architecture, its fashionable bars and shops and its array of
theatres showing the latest musical comedy alongside
classic and experimental theatre, the area has been
favoured by the elite since at least Roman times, due to its
position upwind from the poorer neighbourhoods of the city.

For more than one hundred years it has been known as
Theatreland due to the countless plays performed in the
area. Many shows in London's West End Theatres run
for years, catering to tourists from around the world. *Les
Misérables* has been running since 1985, but the record
holder is *The Mousetrap* by Agatha Christie which has been
running since 1952 and recently celebrated its 26,000th
performance.

QUESTIONS

It's on the Map

1 | Can you locate a major street that shares its name with a word for a piece of hair?

2 | Can you find the name of a green precious stone on the map?

3 | The name of a large Italian island, located in the Mediterranean Sea, can be found on the map. What is it?

Cryptic Challenges

4 | Can you find some summer trousers?

5 | Which street sounds like a great place for supplying beaches?

6 | Where on the map could be heard to be useful for someone wanting candles with large flames?

The Knowledge

7 | What was the title of the 1987 film, starring Anne Bancroft and Anthony Hopkins, about a friendship between an American book lover and a British book store manager? Can you find the location on the map that features in its title?

8 | Which Dickensian novel, first published in full in 1848, centres on a shipping firm? Can you identify the street on the map that shares a name from its title?

9 | Which capital of a group of islands in the Atlantic Ocean, not far off the southeast coast of the United States, was formerly known as Charles Town? Can you find a road on the map that carries its current name?

MAP 24

London Zoo
London, England

Zoological gardens

In between Regents Park and the leafy district of Primrose Hill, London Zoo is perhaps the most famous zoo in the world. It is also the world's oldest, opening in 1828; it was originally a collection for scientific study. It finally opened to the public in 1847, and now houses nearly 700 different species of animal – though its larger animals such as elephants and rhinos have been moved to a more spacious facility outside of London.

London Zoo was bombed several times during the Second World War but although no animals were harmed or escaped, all the venomous animals in the zoo were killed by staff as a precaution.

In 2016 a gorilla escaped from its enclosure and drank several litres of blackcurrant squash in its keeper's room. A more successful escape took place in the 1960s when Goldie the golden eagle escaped from London Zoo and roamed the city for twelve days, memorably killing and eating a duck that belonged to the American ambassador.

QUESTIONS

It's on the Map

1 | Can you identify a road that shares its name with a fictional bear, known for his love of marmalade sandwiches?

2 | The name of the legendary author of the *Iliad* and the *Odyssey* can be found on the map on two parallel streets. Where?

3 | Can you find three words on the map that mean, in turn, 'wide', 'ahead of schedule' and 'a secure place'?

Cryptic Challenges

4 | What might you plug a USB cable into?

5 | Can you find what sounds like a grassy feature for men?

6 | Can you identify a feature on the map that could be heard to be a location for large-scale rubbish disposal?

The Knowledge

7 | Which 'Guy' (not marked on the map) has a statue in his honour near the entrance to London Zoo?

8 | Which English architect, born in 1752, was noted for his work on the development of the area once known as Marylebone Park into what is now Regent's Park? Can you find his surname on the map?

9 | Madame Tussauds waxworks appears on the map (C5), but what is the largest statue (not marked on the map) they have ever made?

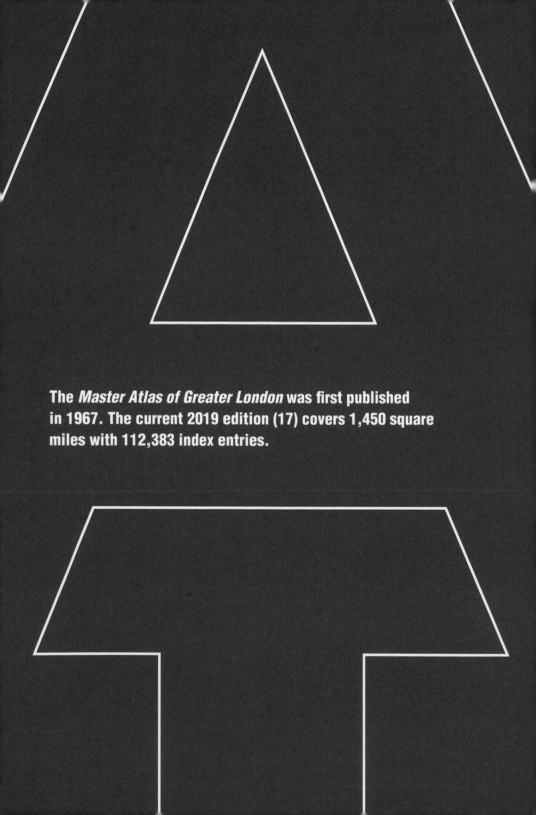

The *Master Atlas of Greater London* was first published in 1967. The current 2019 edition (17) covers 1,450 square miles with 112,383 index entries.

MAP 25

Harry Potter Studio Tour Leavesden, London, England

Film studio and tourist attraction

The Harry Potter movies were among the most successful and the most expensive ever to be made in the UK. They starred the great and the good of British cinema and pushed the technical abilities of film-making and special effects to the limit. Much of the magic was made at the Warner Bros. Studios in Leavesden.

The Leavesden studio was originally an aircraft factory and airfield that played a vital role in aeroplane production in the Second World War. The studios now provide more than 50,000 square metres (538,196 square feet) of space for film production, including one of the largest filtered and heated stage-based water tanks in Europe.

In 2012 after a decade of filming the Harry Potter movies at Leavesden, two studios on the site were opened as a permanent exhibition featuring some of the most iconic sets from the films, from Hogwarts to Diagon Alley.

QUESTIONS

It's on the Map

1 | Can you find the name of a popular team sport on the map?

2 | Can you identify a thoroughfare that shares its name with a heavenly body with an elliptical orbit?

3 | Can you identify two locations on the map that share their names with countries in the Middle East?

Cryptic Challenges

4 | Can you find a location on the map whose name sounds like a place with unfamiliar customs?

5 | An equitable-sounding route can be found. Where is it?

6 | Can you locate what could be interpreted as an environmentally friendly financial institution?

The Knowledge

7 | Which Roman mythological hero, known for his strength, has a name that is also the middle name of a noted English singer and pianist born in 1947? He can be found on the map.

8 | Which actor (not marked on the map) plays the role of Rubeus Hagrid in the Harry Potter movie series, much of which was filmed at Leavesden Film Studios (C2)?

9 | Which former English RAF officer is credited with single-handedly inventing the turbojet engine? Can you find a road that shares his surname?

MAP 26

Royal Shakespeare Theatre Stratford-upon-Avon, England

Theatre

In William Shakespeare's hometown of Stratford-upon-Avon in the English Midlands, the Royal Shakespeare Company operate the Royal Shakespeare Theatre, a 1,000-seater venue in which the works of the great Bard are performed all year round.

On the banks of the River Avon, opposite the town's cricket and recreation grounds, and just a few streets from Shakespeare's birthplace, the theatre was first built in 1879 to celebrate England's greatest playwright. The first theatre was destroyed by fire in 1926 and the current building was completed in 1932. It was designed by Elizabeth Scott and became one of the first buildings in Britain to be constructed from the plans of a female architect. It was redeveloped in 2010 and now forms part of a complex including rehearsal space, a riverside café and a rooftop restaurant.

QUESTIONS

It's on the Map

1 | Can you find two streets on the map that are each named after different farm animals?

2 | Can you find three map locations that all have names that suggest you could moor a ship there?

3 | Can you locate a road that shares its name with a Californian national park, famous for its extremely tall trees?

Cryptic Challenges

4 | Can you find a promising place for Christmas greenery?

5 | Can you find a location that, with a single vowel change, becomes the surname of a leading British rock guitarist?

6 | Which road sounds like a place for an expensive shopping experience?

The Knowledge

7 | Which map feature is an 1888 tribute to Shakespeare? He is seen sitting on a pedestal, surrounded by statues of four of his best-known characters.

8 | Which town, that shares its name with a US state capital, is the fictional location of a long-running US animated TV series? Can you find a road on the map that shares its name?

9 | Which feature on the map shares its name (without the definite article) with the title of a Chekhov play about a family in decline, first published and performed in 1904?

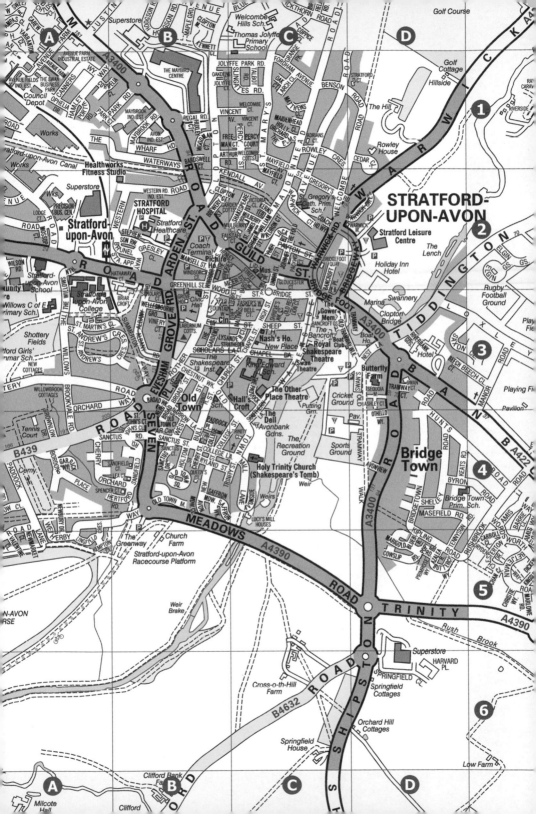

A-Z were the official
paper map supplier to
London 2012, the Games
of the XXX Olympiad.

MAP 27

Glastonbury
Somerset, England

Village

The village of Glastonbury sits above the Somerset Levels in South West England. For centuries it has been associated with spirituality, mysticism and magic. It lays claim to being the birth place of King Arthur, and perhaps the site of Avalon, the legendary island that features in Arthurian myths. Its main feature is Glastonbury Tor, a hill and tower visible for miles around. The Tor is believed by some to form a key part of the Glastonbury Zodiac which is a gargantuan astrological map carved into the earth around the village.

Another major site is the ruins of Glastonbury Abbey which was once one of the most important religious centres in the country and saw the coronation of King Edmund Ironside in 1016. It also features a holy thorn bush that is believed to have been planted by Joseph of Arimathea when he fled Palestine after Jesus' crucifixion. There is a persistent myth that Joseph also brought the Holy Grail to Glastonbury and many people have searched for it.

Glastonbury is also known world-wide for the music festival it lends its name to – The Glastonbury Festival of Performing Arts is the largest green-field festival in the world, but it actually takes place in the nearby village of Pilton. Locals call it the Pilton Pop Festival.

QUESTIONS

It's on the Map

1 | Can you find a road on the map that shares its name with a percussive musical instrument?

2 | A brown spice can be found on the map. Can you locate it?

3 | Can you find the name of a mammal and its young on the map?

Cryptic Challenges

4 | Can you find the same holy cup in three different grid squares?

5 | Which street sounds like a great place for white-collar crime?

6 | Can you locate a street that, in a particular context, could be renamed as '47 Street'?

The Knowledge

7 | According to legend, who was the father of King Arthur? Can you find a location that shares part of his name?

8 | What name for an island in Arthurian legend was also the title of a bestselling album by Roxy Music, in the early 1980s? The name appears on the map.

9 | Which English actress, born in 1979, starred with Ben Affleck in a critically acclaimed 2014 psychological thriller, based on a novel by Gillian Flynn? Can you find her surname on the map?

MAP 28

Chester Zoo
Cheshire, England

Zoological gardens

One of the largest zoos in the UK, Chester Zoo is the most visited wildlife attraction in the country. It was founded by George Mottershead in 1931 after he took a trip to Manchester Zoo and was shocked by the cramped and unsanitary conditions for the animals there. He decided to create a zoo without bars that provided appropriate habitats for the animals, and Chester Zoo still uses an array of moats and ditches rather than cages. In 1956 chimpanzees were released onto islands in the zoo, with only 3.7 metres (12 feet) of water between them and the public. At the time it was not known if chimps could swim, luckily it turned out they could not.

Rhinos, tigers, jaguars, parrots, buffalo, elephants and orangutans are all residents of the zoo today, and can be viewed from a mile-long monorail that runs around the park.

QUESTIONS

It's on the Map

1 | Can you identify a road that shares its name with a word that can mean 'healthy'?

2 | The surname of a 1970s prime minister can be found on the map in two road names. What are they?

3 | How many times does the name 'Newton' appear on the map? Only count the word if all of its letters are fully inside the coloured area of the map.

Cryptic Challenges

4 | Which word on the map is to fill someone with wonder and delight?

5 | What two-word street name might give you hope if you were looking for an ATM?

6 | Which road sounds prone to traffic jams?

The Knowledge

7 | Which ruined abbey, located by a village on the Welsh bank of the River Wye, was founded in 1131 by Walter de Clare? Can you find a road that shares its name?

8 | Which English actress, born in 1964, had a leading role in a 2013 Scottish musical film directed by Dexter Fletcher? Can you pinpoint a thoroughfare that shares her surname?

9 | What type of animal (not found on the map) was Jubilee, born at Chester Zoo in 1977, and named in celebration of the Queen's Silver Jubilee year?

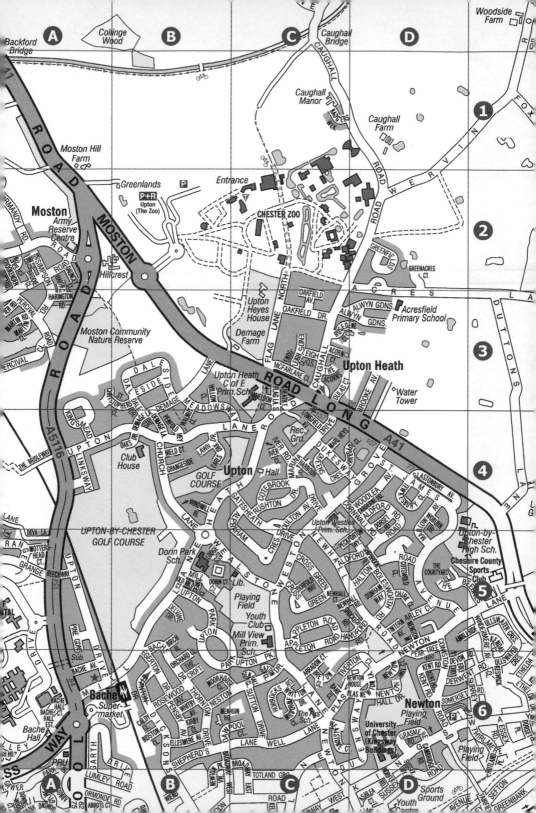

The most common street name in the A-Z database is High Street with 2,341 entries. This is followed by Church Lane (1,966) and Station Road (1,919).

MAP 29

Blackpool
Lancashire, England

Seaside resort

For generations the word Blackpool has been synonymous with sunshine and seaside holidays. Famous for its beach and the Blackpool Tower, people first began taking their holidays in Blackpool in the 1700s and by the early twentieth century it was one of the most popular destinations in the world. Today it still welcomes more than eighteen million tourists every year.

Blackpool's main draw has always been its seven-mile sandy beach, but it also boasts attractions including the Pleasure Beach amusement park, the three piers, Madame Tussaud's waxwork exhibition, the Winter Gardens and the world famous Blackpool Illuminations. The Illuminations have been taking place since the late nineteenth century and last for sixty-six days each year. They involve huge light displays and more than a million bulbs.

Blackpool also has the UK's only surviving first generation tramway. Built in 1885, it still carries millions of passengers each year and has a selection of rare double-decker trams.

QUESTIONS

It's on the Map

1 | Can you find three locations on the map that share their names with different titles of British aristocracy?

2 | Can you identify a feature on the map that shares its name with a two-term, twentieth-century US president?

3 | The name of a South American bird of the vulture family can be found on the map. Where?

Cryptic Challenges

4 | Can you find something added to a pizza or a cake?

5 | Where might you see female royalty on display?

6 | Can you locate what sounds like a male company director?

The Knowledge

7 | Which location, featured on the map and first opened to the public in 1894, was inspired by the Eiffel Tower in Paris?

8 | Which British painter was responsible for *The Blue Boy*, a full-length oil portrait that was first exhibited in 1779? Can you find a feature on the map that bears his surname?

9 | Which Blackpool entertainment venue, first opened in 1878, has hosted many big names from the world of showbusiness, along with annual party political conferences?

MAP 30

Kelvingrove Museum Glasgow, Scotland

Art gallery and museum

The Kelvingrove Art Gallery and Museum sits in the leafy West End of Glasgow, below the tower of Glasgow University, in Kelvingrove Park. It is situated between the River Kelvin and the River Clyde and its red sandstone towers can be seen from across the city.

The museum was built in a Spanish baroque style as part of the Glasgow International Exhibition of 1901. Its centre hall features an enormous pipe organ made up of more than 2,800 pipes, which holds the record for the longest-running daily organ recital in the world, having been played on 3,000 consecutive days by musicians including the organists of the Whitehouse and of Christchurch Cathedral in New Zealand.

Among the collections belonging to the museum are many pictures by great artists from Da Vinci to Rennie Mackintosh. But the most famous exhibit is Dali's masterpiece *Christ of St John of the Cross*. This surreal perspective on the crucifixion is seen by millions of people each year.

QUESTIONS

It's on the Map

1 | How many car parks are marked with symbols on the map?

2 | Can you identify a street that shares its name with a term for a match between two rival sports teams from the same area?

3 | Can you find the name of a large-clawed mammal, known for its plated body covering?

Cryptic Challenges

4 | There is a word on the map that, if split in two, could describe a man who is smartly dressed. What word is it?

5 | Which location on the map sounds like a great place for buying bakery items?

6 | Can you find a House with a Speaker and Senate?

The Knowledge

7 | Which Met Office shipping forecast area is named after a captain on Charles Darwin's voyage aboard HMS *Beagle*? Can you locate a feature on the map that shares his surname?

8 | Which surrealist artist (not marked on the map) painted the picture entitled *Christ of St John of the Cross*, that first went on display in the Kelvingrove Art Gallery and Museum in 1952?

9 | Which nineteenth-century British prime minister was described by Florence Nightingale as follows: 'Though he made a joke when asked to do the right thing, he always did it'? Can you find a location on the map that shares the name in his aristocratic title?

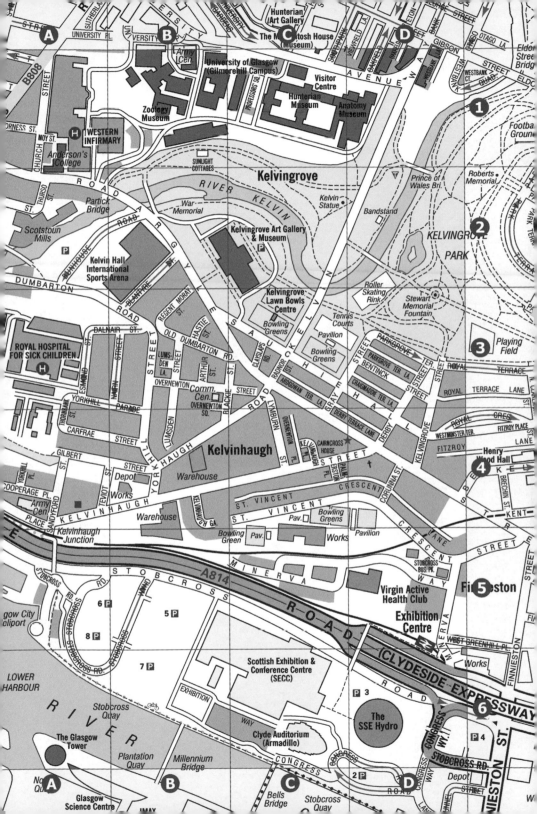

TRANSPORT

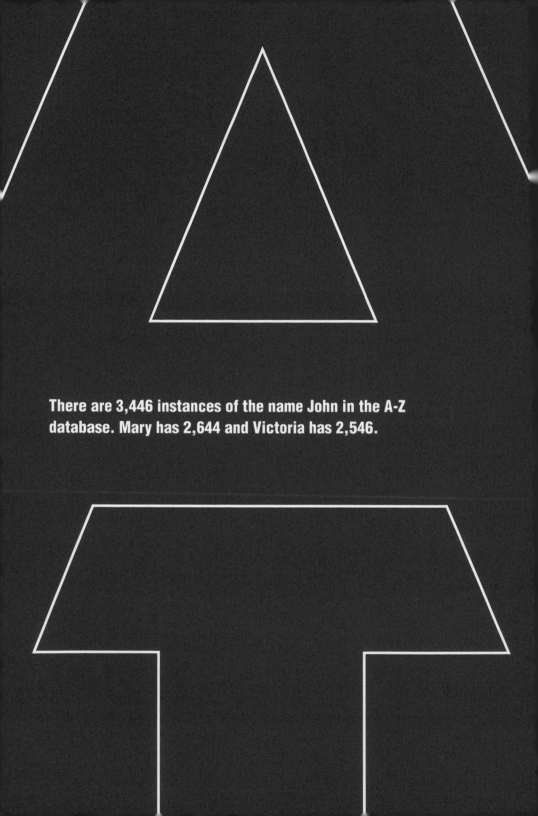

There are 3,446 instances of the name John in the A-Z database. Mary has 2,644 and Victoria has 2,546.

MAP 31

Heathrow Airport
London, England

Airport

The busiest airport in Europe and second busiest passenger airport in the world, London Heathrow International Airport was founded as an airfield in 1929 at a time when the area was made up of the orchards and market gardens around Heathrow Hall and Heathrow Farm.

Heathrow became the main airport for London in 1946 and since then has continued to grow, with two runways, five terminals, and more than 80 million passengers a year. The airport is also a major shopping centre, with a bottle of Chanel Nº5 sold in Heathrow on average every five minutes. You may be familiar with terminals one to five, but there is a small 'terminal six' that is reserved for VIPs and contains the Royal Suite for the use of the Royal Family.

Much controversy has surrounded the proposed construction of a third runway at Heathrow, and the economic benefits and environmental costs have been debated in parliament and in camps of climate activists around the airport.

QUESTIONS

It's on the Map

1 | Can you identify a road that shares its name with a natural meteorological phenomenon? And then another road which is a man-made meteorological phenomenon?

2 | Can you find the names of three birds on the map? One is quite obscure, however.

3 | There is a cocktail hiding somewhere on the map, although one of its letters has been deleted to save space. Can you spot it even so?

Cryptic Challenges

4 | Can you identify a word on the map whose name sounds like two words meaning 'trapped joint'?

5 | Can you find a place on the map that starts with a common fast-food item?

6 | There is a 'monstrous' road on the map. Can you find it?

The Knowledge

7 | Which Scottish town is the port that provided the first roll-on roll-off ferry services between the British mainland and Ireland? Can you find a location on the map that bears its name?

8 | Which monster in Greek mythology was a supernatural female creature with her heads on snaky necks and her loins bearing the heads of baying dogs? Can you find a feature that bears its name?

9 | According to figures from 2017, which terminal at Heathrow Airport had the largest volume of passengers and flights?

MAP 32

Waterloo
London, England

Train station

The terminus of the South Western Main Line and a stop
on the Bakerloo, Jubilee, Northern, Waterloo and City lines
of the London Underground; Waterloo Station is the second
busiest station in the UK and the largest, with twenty-four
platforms. Built in 1928, it was the last London Terminus to
run a steam service, and was also the first station to run
the Eurostar to Paris until the line was transferred over to
St Pancras in 2007. Briefly privatised between 1994 and
2002, Waterloo station is today owned and managed by the
publicly owned company Network Rail.

The station is near major attractions including London
County Hall, the London Eye, Royal Festival Hall and the
Southbank. It sits within the borough of Lambeth. As well as
overground and underground trains, the station also serves
as a terminus of buses, and boats at the nearby London
Eye Pier.

QUESTIONS

It's on the Map

1 | Can you find the name of a fruit on the map?

2 | Can you pinpoint a feature on the map that shares its name with a machine that can crush grain or convert the power of wind into electricity?

3 | The name of a fermented alcoholic drink can be found on the map. What is it?

Cryptic Challenges

4 | Which word can have its middle letters swapped to create a term synonymous with Shakespeare?

5 | Which street on the map sounds like it might contain mouldy meat?

6 | Can you find a fat fortification?

The Knowledge

7 | Which location on the map commemorates a British victory over Napoleon and has counterparts in Paris and New York?

8 | Which fictional British detective made his first literary appearance in *Beeton's Christmas Annual* of 1887? Can you find a feature on the map that shares his name?

9 | Waterloo Station is the busiest station in the UK, with 100 million passengers per year. How many platforms does it have?

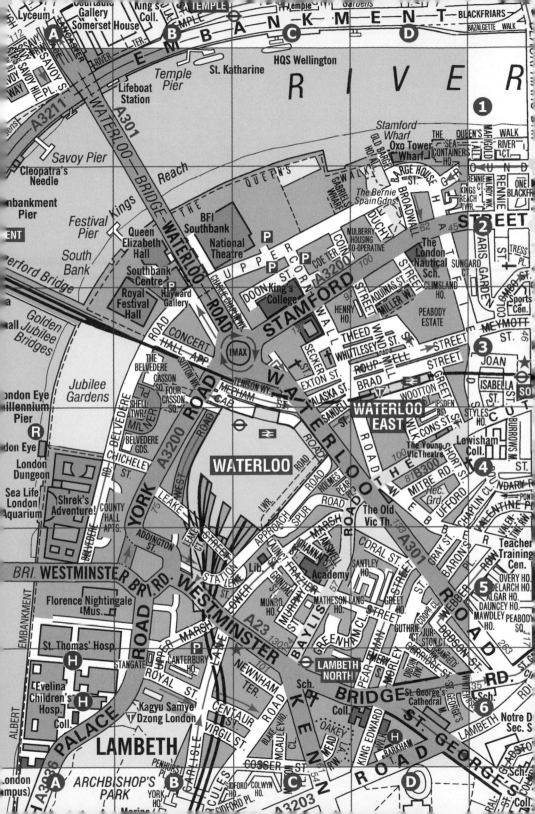

The longest town name in the A-Z database is
Llanfairpwllgwyngyllgogerychwyrndrobwllllantysiliogogogoch
on the island of Anglesey, although it is shown in its short form,
Llanfair Pwllgwyngyll, on the map.

MAP 33

Euston/King's Cross London, England

Train stations

Euston, King's Cross and St Pancras Stations are major London terminuses for the East Coast Main Line, the West Coast Main Line and the Eurostar respectively. All located within a small area of the London borough of Camden, they make up one of the most significant areas of rail infrastructure in the UK.

Euston was the first intercity station in London and was built by George and Robert Stephenson, who are considered by many to be the fathers of the railway. The station at first served a line to Birmingham, but now allows passengers to continue north to Liverpool, Glasgow and Fort William.

King's Cross runs long-distance trains to Edinburgh and Glasgow, and was the terminal station for famous locomotives such as the *Mallard* and the *Flying Scotsman*. The station is also well known for its association with the Harry Potter books and is the site of the fictional Platform 9¾ where young witches and wizards can catch the *Hogwarts Express*.

QUESTIONS

It's on the Map

1 | Can you identify a feature on the map that shares its name with a wild cat?

2 | Can you find a road that shares its name with a place for keeping horses, and which sounds like a safe place to visit?

3 | The names of two different shapes can be found on the map – but where?

Cryptic Challenges

4 | Can you find a fast-moving location?

5 | Where could you observe the use of a medieval weapon beneath a type of architecture?

6 | Can you identify a word on the map that sounds like somewhere you might find a beach?

The Knowledge

7 | Which US state capital shares its name with a mythical bird? Can you identify two features on the map that bear this name?

8 | Which German-born classical composer is noted for a piece of music designed for a royal concert held in 1717 on the River Thames? Can you find his name on the map?

9 | Which Newcastle-born civil engineer, whose surname can be found on the map, was known as the 'Father of the Railways'?

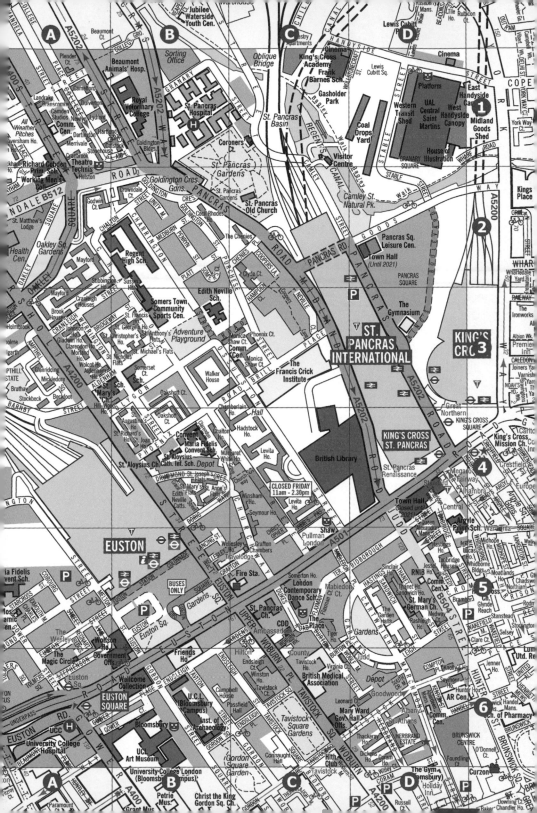

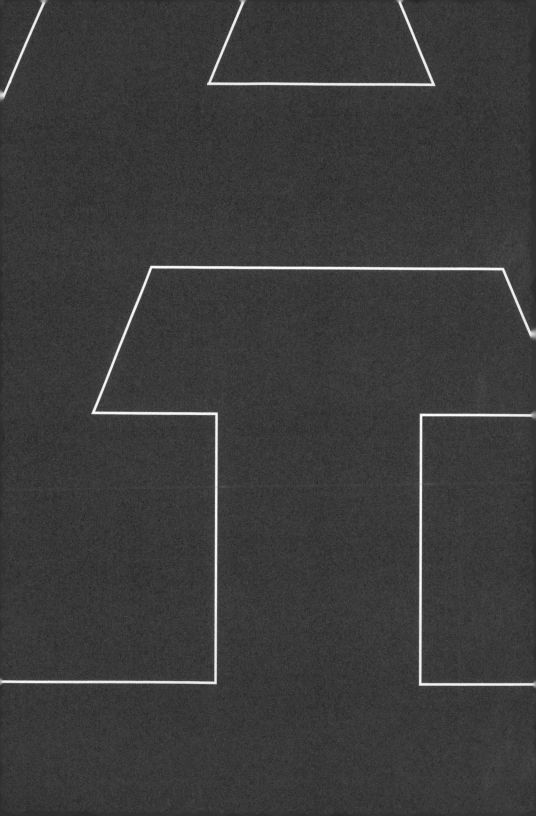

MAP 34

Victoria Coach Station
London, England

Bus and coach station

On Buckingham Palace Road in Central London, the Victoria Coach Station has, since 1932, been the main point of arrival for millions of people visiting London each year. The station is an imposing art deco structure just a few minutes' walk from Victoria main line and Underground Stations, the Royal Mews and Buckingham Palace.

The station sits on the border between Belgravia and Pimlico and is a valuable piece of real estate, operated by Transport for London, but owned by the Duke of Westminster. In 2013 the duke announced that he intended to demolish the building and relocate the coach station elsewhere in the city, but the building was quickly listed as Grade II by English Heritage.

The coach station stretches around the older Victoria Library which though bombed in the Second World War still retains many Victorian features.

QUESTIONS

It's on the Map

1 | Can you locate the name of an ornamental water feature on the map?

2 | There is a word on the map that refers to both a high-ranking priest and a type of number. What is it?

3 | Where on the map has a name that sounds like an appropriate place to keep a pet budgerigar?

Cryptic Challenges

4 | Can you find a feature that sounds like (and yet isn't) a great place to fill up with petrol?

5 | There is what sounds like an item of environmentally friendly clothing on the map. Can you find it?

6 | Where on the map might you find 'an American expression'?

The Knowledge

7 | Which Australian state capital is named after an Earl of Buckinghamshire? Can you find a feature on the map that shares its name?

8 | Which English poet produced an allegorical poem about the Elizabethan dynasty that was published with the help of Sir Walter Raleigh? Can you identify a location that shares his surname?

9 | 'Victoria' tube station contains three different vowels (with one repeated). Can you name the only two stations on the London Underground that contain all five vowels? They are not on the map.

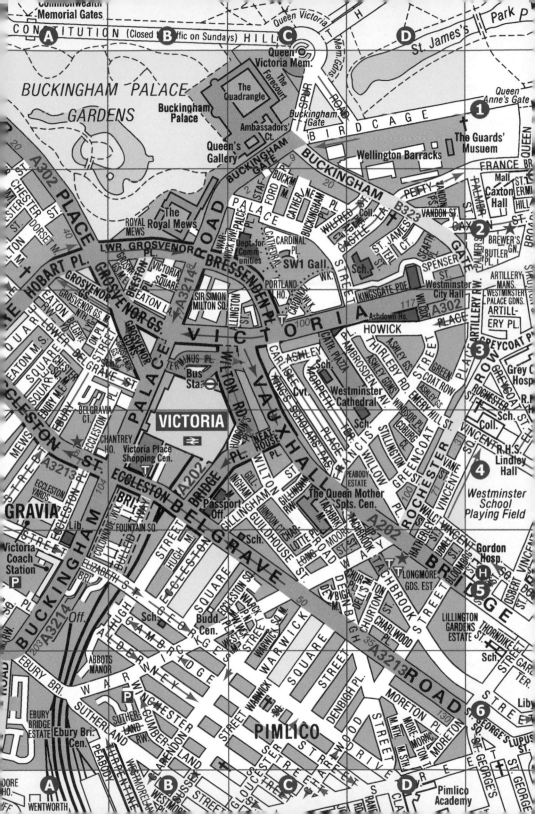

One of the most unusual addresses recorded in the A-Z database is 'Second Star on the Right and Straight on 'til Morning' which is in 'Land of Green Ginger', Kingston upon Hull.

MAP 35

Portsmouth Harbour
Hampshire, England

Train station, port and tourist attraction

Since pre-Roman times the large natural harbour at Portsmouth has been a major military and commercial asset on the Solent. The harbour today is enclosed by Portsea Island and Gosport and hosts a range of naval installations, ancient maritime vessels, ferry terminals, a train station and the University of Portsmouth. The harbour itself contains several islands, including Whale Island which is home of the naval training base HMS *Excellent*.

It is possible to travel from Portsmouth harbour by ferry to the Isle of Wight, the Channel Islands, France and Spain. The harbour is also the home port for the Royal Navy's Super Carriers the HMS *Queen Elizabeth* and HMS *Prince of Wales*.

The harbour also contains Portsmouth Historic Dockyard which is open to the public and contains a number of significant historic ships including HMS *M33*, a First World War vessel; HMS *Warrior*, the world's first armour-plated ship; and HMS *Victory*, Horatio Nelson's flagship which has been open to the public for more than two hundred years.

QUESTIONS

It's on the Map

1 | Can you find the name of two current British coins on the map, one of which is in the plural, along with the name of a pre-decimal British coin too?

2 | Can you pinpoint a feature on the map that shares its name with that of a Roman soldier?

3 | Two different big cats can be found on the map. Can you locate them both? And then can you find two further streets that have the same name as one of them?

Cryptic Challenges

4 | Can you find a brief argument?

5 | A 'series of waterfalls' can be found on the map. Where?

6 | Where on the map appears to tell the story of an army's withdrawal?

The Knowledge

7 | Which location on the map commemorates a battleship owned by Henry VIII that sank in 1545 and was eventually recovered in 1982?

8 | Which English cricket ground hosted England's 1,000th test match in 2018? Can you find a location on the map that shares its name?

9 | Which two Spanish cities can be reached directly by ferry from Portsmouth?

MAP 36

Dover
Kent, England

Town and harbour

As the point of arrival or departure for many British people travelling for holidays, emigration or war, the Port of Dover, with its castle and white cliffs, has taken on a hugely symbolic position in the public imagination and is woven into the idea of Britain as an island nation.

Dover itself is a small town facing France over the narrowest part of the English Channel. It has been a port for millennia, and its name derives from the Brythonic word for water, which was Latinised to read as Dubris by the Romans. It has been called Dover since at least Shakespearean times, and in the play *King Lear* the character of Gloucester threatens to throw himself from the White Cliffs of Dover.

In 1940 Dover played a major role in Operation Dynamo, the evacuation of Dunkirk. Directed from Dover Castle and using many small boats from the harbour, more than 300,000 Allied soldiers were rescued from Dunkirk as the German Army advanced on them. A monument to the event stands at the centre of the docks.

QUESTIONS

It's on the Map

1 | Can you find two contemporary British royals on the map? One is written in abbreviated form in a circle.

2 | The name of a sea-dwelling mammal can be found on the map, although a final vowel has been deleted for space. What is it?

3 | Can you locate a group of policemen on the map?

Cryptic Challenges

4 | Where on the map sounds like it might be useful for stopping cattle escaping?

5 | Can you identify a word on the map that, if its first letter was changed, would be the name of an Australian state capital?

6 | Can you find a large 'bargain'?

The Knowledge

7 | Which feature on the map commemorates a French pilot, born in 1872, who performed a noted aviation first?

8 | Which knighted English painter, a founder of the Pre-Raphaelite Brotherhood, is particularly noted for a painting of a Shakespearean heroine floating in a river? A feature on the map shares his name.

9 | Which American actress, born in 1979, has the lead role in a popular US TV series about intelligence operations that first appeared in 2011? Can you identify the location that shares her surname?

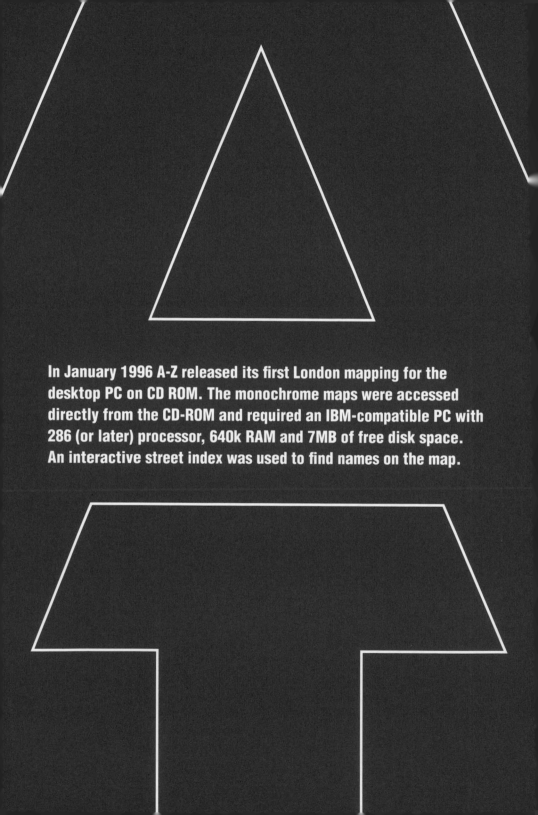

In January 1996 A-Z released its first London mapping for the desktop PC on CD ROM. The monochrome maps were accessed directly from the CD-ROM and required an IBM-compatible PC with 286 (or later) processor, 640k RAM and 7MB of free disk space. An interactive street index was used to find names on the map.

MAP 37

Birmingham New Street
Birmingham, England

Train station

Birmingham New Street is the sixth busiest train station in the UK, and the busiest interchange outside London, with almost seven million passengers changing trains at the station each year, and forty-three million passengers getting on and off.

The station was first built in 1846, but its famous redevelopment in the 1960s gave it its distinctive brutalist design. By 2003 it had been voted 'the second biggest eyesore in the UK' and a major redevelopment began – it is now a vast modern building incorporating parts of the Victorian and brutalist designs. Still often considered one of the least-loved train stations in Britain, its near neighbour Birmingham Moor Street has often been voted one of the prettiest stations in the country.

QUESTIONS

It's on the Map

1 | Can you find a road on the map that shares its name with a swift-flying bird with a forked tail?

2 | Where on the map might you find the name of part of a duck's anatomy?

3 | Can you identify a thoroughfare that shares its name with an Italian city?

Cryptic Challenges

4 | Can you find a useless street?

5 | Where on the map might you find what sounds like a doctor's potential description of a female patient who turned out not to need treatment?

6 | Which path could you add 'it' to, to form the less populous communities?

The Knowledge

7 | Which former mayor of Birmingham was the father of a British prime minister? Can you identify a feature on the map that bears their surname?

8 | Which footballer scored the goal that prompted the noted piece of TV commentary, 'They think it's all over… It is now!'? Can you find a street that shares his surname?

9 | If you have a train ticket for 'Birmingham Stns' (Birmingham Stations), which three city centre stations can you get off or on at?

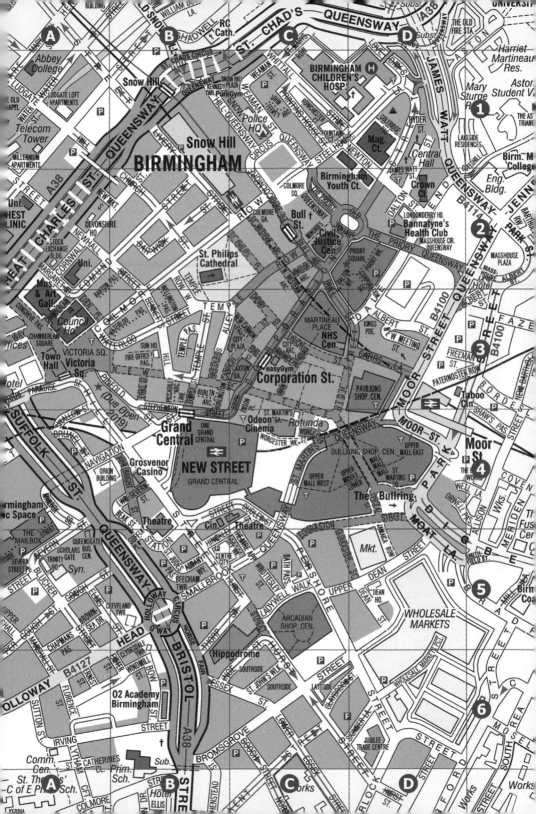

MAP 38

M6/M42 Junction
The Midlands, England

Motorway junction

The M42 runs from Bromsgrove in Worcestershire to
Ashby-de-la-Zouch in Leicestershire, serving the eastern
side of Birmingham. The M6 runs from Rugby to Gretna,
crossing most of England and connecting to the M1.
The two meet at junction 4 of the M6 on the outskirts of
Birmingham, not far from the National Exhibition Centre,
Birmingham Airport, the National Motorcycle Museum and
the hamlet of Little Packington. The area is low-lying and
contains a number of ponds and lakes.

The M6 was constructed in 1959 and the M42 was added
thirty years later. Between them the two roads have
transformed what was once a farming community some
miles from the edge of Birmingham into an extremely busy
transport route serving the Midlands.

QUESTIONS

It's on the Map

1 | Can you identify a thoroughfare on the map that shares its name with a current currency?.

2 | There are four features on the map that share their names with flowers. Can you find them all?

3 | Can you locate two roads that share their names with the surnames of two different British prime ministers?

Cryptic Challenges

4 | Which location sounds extremely vulpine?

5 | Can you identify a feature on the map that, if its third letter was changed, could become a moving part in a car engine?

6 | Can you find a sharp piece of mineral?

The Knowledge

7 | Can you find the name of Aquaman's signature weapon on the map, as described by the DC Comics Universe?

8 | Which famous explorer of the Elizabethan period had a fleet of five ships whose original names were *Pelican*, *Elizabeth*, *Marigold*, *Swan* and *Benedict*? Can you find the location on the map that shares his surname?

9 | When the first section of the M42 was opened in the 1970s, what facility became directly linked to the M6 for the first time?

Copyright protection measures are often used by map makers, including A-Z, to identify any unauthorized copying or similar misuse. These devices can include minor changes or insignificant additions to the map and are often referred to as 'Trap Streets' or 'Phantom Names'. A-Z's most elaborate example of protection was a series of dots positioned across London that, when joined together, revealed the A-Z logo.

MAP 39

Sheffield Supertram
Sheffield, England

Tram network

In the South Yorkshire city of Sheffield, work began on a new cutting-edge tram system in the 1980s. One of the earliest of the new generation of trams, the Sheffield Supertram promised to be a light rail network for the modern city. Completed by 1994, the tram network connected areas of new track with underused heavy rail lines and provided a new public transport option in Sheffield. But initial interest was slow and limited services combined with a complex ticketing system resulted in disappointing passenger numbers in its early years.

However over time usage of the Supertram has more than doubled, and the line has been extended several times. Today more than fifteen million people use the service every year and there are plans to extend the Supertram to other towns and cities in South Yorkshire.

QUESTIONS

It's on the Map

1 | Can you identify a road on the map that shares its name with both a tree and its fruit? It is also the name of a luxury fashion brand.

2 | Can you find a building on the map that shares its exact name with another building of the same function in London, but does not contain a brand in its name?

3 | The name of a Greek island can be found on the map. Which island is it?

Cryptic Challenges

4 | Can you find three words on the map that could each be anagrammed as one of the following? Ignore the added spaces.

    a | Wet again
    b | More trim
    c | Spare note

5 | Can you identify a feature on the map that, if one letter was changed, would form the surname of one of the Beatles?

6 | An argument about the Lord's Prayer can be found on the map. Where?

The Knowledge

7 | What feature on the map, also a term for a melting pot, has been the regular venue for a major sporting world championship since 1977?

8 | Which early twenty-first-century US vice president also served as a congressman for Wyoming for ten years? Can you find a feature on the map that shares his surname?

9 | What colours are used on maps of the four lines that cover the fifty stations served by the Sheffield Supertram?

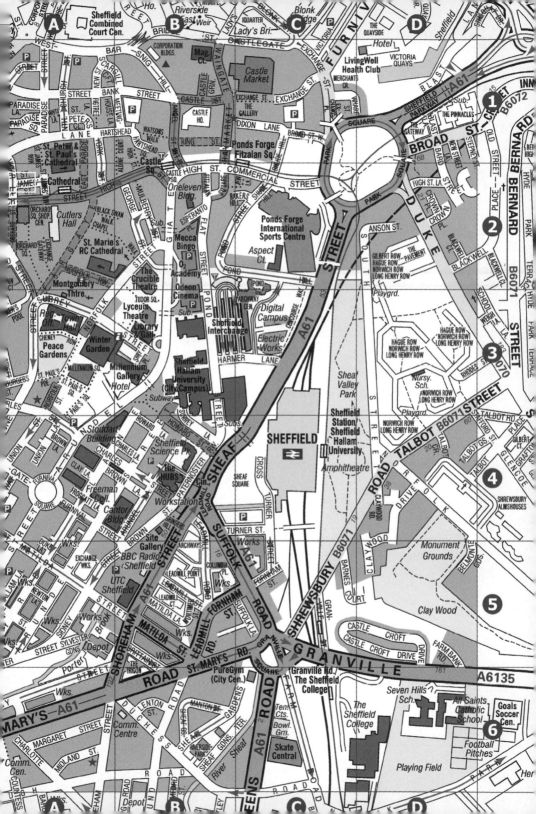

MAP 40

Mancunian Way
Manchester, England

Elevated motorway

Cutting through central Manchester and constituting part of the city's inner ring road, the Mancunian Way is a two-mile stretch of raised motorway that runs east to west across the city from the neighbourhoods of Hulme and Moss Side. It crosses the campuses of Manchester's two universities and bisects Oxford Road, which is well known as Manchester's Curry Mile.

The Mancunian Way was the UK's second aerial flyover and the first to be built outside London. It is made of precast concrete with a hollow-box spine. In 1961, before construction, a 1/12th scale model of the Mancunian Way was built to stress test the design.

In 2015, after incredibly high rainfall in Manchester, a sink hole caused parts of the eastern section of the Mancunian Way to collapse. The stretch of road remained closed for nearly a year.

QUESTIONS

It's on the Map

1 | Can you find the names of six birds on the map?

2 | Can you find a road on the map that share its name with a brass musical instrument?

3 | The name of a continent can be found on the map, just next to the name of a country within that continent. Can you find them?

Cryptic Challenges

4 | Which street sounds like somewhere that good games behaviour is required?

5 | Can you find an angry road?

6 | Where might you expect to find Manhattan on this map?

The Knowledge

7 | Which gallery, featured on the map, was founded in 1889 by a prominent Mancunian lawyer and has over 50,000 items in its collection?

8 | Which footballer moved from England for a then-world-record fee to Real Madrid in 2013? Can you identify a feature on the map that shares his surname?

9 | Who was prime minister at the time that Manchester Piccadilly became the name of the city's main train station?

NATURE

The first computer used in A-Z map production was introduced in the mid-1980s, complete with a monochrome or 'green screen' VDU. The operator typed street names and other map text into the computer which recorded the data on punched tape media. In a second stage the punched tape was transferred to a reader to output either as ready-to-apply map text or a finished index on film.

MAP 41

Hyde Park
London, England
Public park

The largest of the Royal Parks in Central London that form
a chain through the city to Buckingham Palace, Hyde Park
has long been a focus of both leisure, free speech and
political unrest in the city.

The park was established in 1536 by Henry VIII when he
took the land from Westminster Abbey in his reformation
and used it for hunting. It opened to the public in 1637, and
its two lakes, the Serpentine and the Long Water, were
added by Queen Caroline in 1730. It was the site of the
Great Exhibition in 1851 and the original location of the
Crystal Palace. In 1872 Speakers Corner was established
in the park as a place of free speech, debate and radical
dissent and it remains a political gathering place – though
at various times police have intervened to stop speakers on
legal grounds.

QUESTIONS

It's on the Map

1 | Can you identify two roads on the map that both share their name with the same season of the year?

2 | Can you pinpoint a road that shares its name with an Olympic sport?

3 | Can you find a thoroughfare that shares its name with an aromatic herb?

Cryptic Challenges

4 | Can you identify a major street on the map that, if a single vowel was changed, would become a common measure of many drinks?

5 | There is a small, curving road on the map that, if an extra letter was inserted before its current first letter, would denote a central family in the Harry Potter book and film series. What is it?

6 | Can you find the name of a famous poet on the map that, if the middle letter was changed, would instead become a word meaning 'to stay in the air without moving'?

The Knowledge

7 | Which location on the map (marked, but not labelled with its name) was the London townhouse of a preeminent nineteenth-century British military hero and prime minister, and was once known as 'Number 1 London'?

8 | Which feature on the map includes as its centrepiece two bronze figures dancing above a pond?

9 | Which word on the map is the surname of a US actor noted for playing a comic book superhero in a 1950s US TV series; and, without its final letter, also the surname of a different US actor known for playing the same superhero in a later film series?

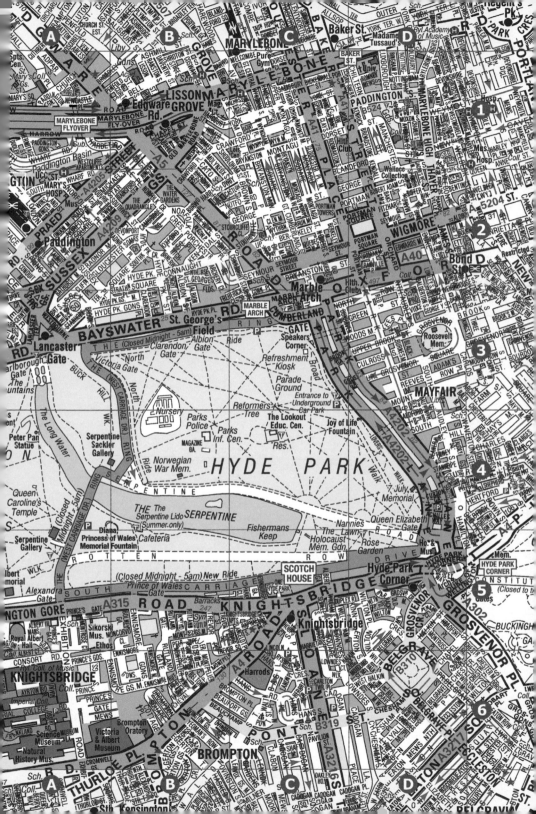

MAP 42

Royal Botanic Gardens at Kew London, England

Botanical gardens and archive

In the far South West of London, Kew Gardens is home to the largest and most diverse botanical collection in the world, containing a plethora of greenhouses, nurseries, arboreta, lakes and follies.

Beginning its life as the exotic garden of Kew Palace, and becoming the Royal Botanic Garden in 1840, Kew is home to more than 30,000 varieties of living plant as well as over seven million preserved plant species. Its library houses 750,000 books and more than 100,000 prints and drawings of plants.

The gardens have their own police force, the Kew Constabulary. Made up of just fourteen officers, it has existed for nearly 200 years and has the same powers as the Metropolitan Police.

Just a few hundred metres from the gardens, all of Britain's documents of state, from cabinet papers to secret service reports are stored at the National Archive.

QUESTIONS

It's on the Map

1 | Can you identify a location that shares its name with a horned animal?

2 | Can you find a feature on the map that shares its name with a type of puzzle?

3 | Twin brothers are said to have founded Rome. Can you find the name of one of them on the map?

4 | Which feature on the map shares its name with the author of *Robinson Crusoe*?

Cryptic Challenges

5 | There is a feature on the map that, if its first letter was changed, would become a common meteorological condition. It is seven letters in length. What is it?

6 | Can you pinpoint a location that, if one letter was changed, could denote a vehicle that is associated with funerals?

7 | Can you solve these cryptic crossword clues, the answers to which are pairs of consecutive words found on the map?

  a | Agitated tail gone in beast container? (4, 4)
  b | Five, is it, or fraction of a dollar with respect to amenity (7, 6)

The Knowledge

8 | Which location once belonged to the wife of a Hanoverian British king?

9 | Which building on the map shares its name with a double winner of the Mercury Music Prize?

10 | Which plant house is the most recent to have opened at Kew Gardens?

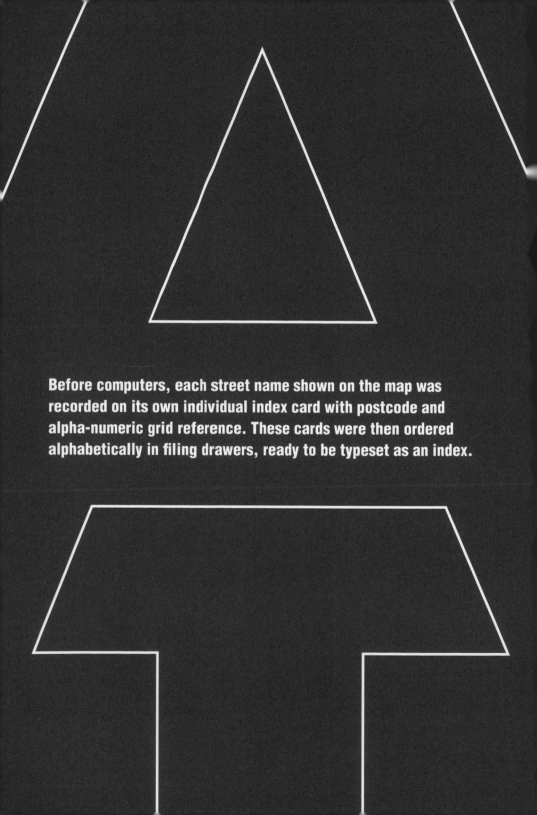

Before computers, each street name shown on the map was recorded on its own individual index card with postcode and alpha-numeric grid reference. These cards were then ordered alphabetically in filing drawers, ready to be typeset as an index.

MAP 43

Hampstead Heath
London, England

Park

One of the highest points in London, Hampstead Heath is
a large grassy ridge overlooking the city, and has been one
of the city's major green spaces since ancient times. Its
name is first recorded in 986 when the area was given by
Ethelred the Unready to one of his servants.

An array of rambling wooded hills make up the heath and
are dotted with a collection of ponds, playgrounds, a
pétanque pitch, a volleyball court, a lido and a training
track. The park also included the estate of the former stately
home, Kenwood House, and is next to Hampstead Golf
Course.

The southern part of the heath is known as parliament hill
and from here the view of London is protected by law. Karl
Marx and his family used to regularly visit the hill as one of
their favourite outings in London.

QUESTIONS

It's on the Map

1 | The name of a Greek god is written on the map, crossing back and forth between the faded yellow section and the main map. Can you find it?

2 | Can you identify a road on the map that shares its name with a wind-direction device? As a hint, it crosses over one of the grid lines.

3 | Can you find a location, not far from one of the occurrences of the word 'Hampstead', that shares its name with an item for holding drinks?

Cryptic Challenges

4 | Can you locate three words that can be anagrammed as each of the following in turn, ignoring the spaces?

      a | Snap raids
      b | Grand frolic
      c | Drew burden

5 | Can you pinpoint a thoroughfare that, if its middle letter was changed, would become the name of a musical keyboard instrument?

6 | Can you find a word on the map where, were its third letter to be changed, it would become a means of transporting oil?

The Knowledge

7 | Which neoclassical villa, used as a venue for summer concerts, houses a collection of Old Master paintings including one of Rembrandt's masterpieces?

8 | Which location on the map commemorates a celebrated English Romantic poet who died in Rome at the age of 25?

9 | Can you find a feature on the map that shares its name with a sportsman who played both football for Arsenal and cricket for Middlesex and England? He also has a stand at Lord's named in his honour.

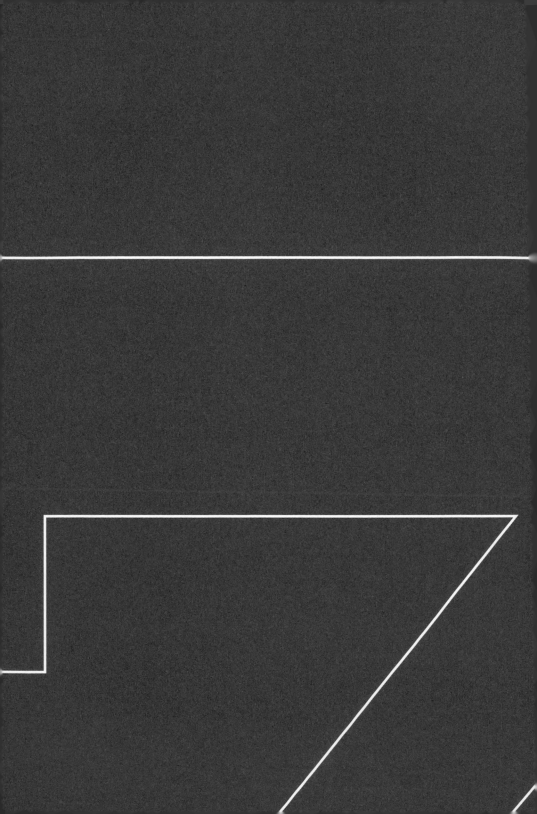

MAP 44

Preston Park
Brighton, England
Park

The lawns and formal gardens of Preston Park are one of the most picturesque areas of Brighton. Located in the north of the town in Preston Village, the park was originally the grounds of Preston Manor.

The park is well known as the site of the rallying ground for the end of the Brighton & Hove Pride Parade. Opposite the park, on the other side of London Road, is The Rockery, the largest municipal rock garden in the UK. The park also has a sensory garden for the blind.

In the northeast corner of the park is Preston Park Velodrome. Opened in 1877, it is the oldest working velodrome in the world.

QUESTIONS

It's on the Map

1 | Can you find the names of ten different trees on the map, either in the singular or plural?

2 | Can you find a sport on the map that has both Union and League variants?

3 | A northern member of the European Union can be found on the map. Which country is it?

Cryptic Challenges

4 | Which road sounds like a warning that a mythical wizard is approaching?

5 | If it took several attempts to get through to someone on the phone, you might have had… what?

6 | Can you find a holy lady who is feeling good?

The Knowledge

7 | What is the capital of the US state whose official nickname is 'The Ocean State'? Can you find it on the map?

8 | Which well-known group of singing brothers, born in Utah, have sold over 77 million records? Can you find their surname on the map?

9 | Which feature on the map covers an underground water source, sometimes known as 'Brighton's lost river'?

In 2006, BBC TWO's *The Culture Show* and the Design Museum conducted a poll to find the nation's favourite example of British design since 1900 – The Great British Design Quest. The *A-Z London Street Atlas* was selected for the public vote finishing in the top twenty-five.

MAP 45

Wollaton Park
Nottingham, England

Park

In the heart of Nottingham, Wollaton Park is a deer park,
stately home and site of the Nottingham Industrial Museum
and Nottingham Natural History Museum. Its 500 acres
were enclosed in the eighteenth century by Barron
Middleton and the creation of the park involved the
destruction of the village of Sutton Passeys.

Containing a school, a lake and Wollaton Hall, the park is a
major leisure ground for the people of Nottingham. As well
as parkland, playing fields and a golf course it has a deer
park that is home to herds of red and fallow deer. Other
wildlife in the park includes rooks, widgeons and a pair of
parakeets.

In the centre of the park the imposing Wollaton Hall is an
Elizabethan house dating from the 1580s. It is now open as
a museum and has been used in filming, most recently as
the Wayne Mansion in the Batman movies.

QUESTIONS

It's on the Map

1 | Can you identify roads on the map that share their names with two different birds?

2 | There is a feature on the map that shares its name with the word for a group of head monks. Can you find it?

3 | Can you locate a street that shares its name with a term for victory?

Cryptic Challenges

4 | Can you find a word on the map that, if its first letter was changed, would refer to something commonly found adjoining a house?

5 | Can you find a road in column C that, if its first vowel was changed, would become the surname of a leading US actor noted for his role in a 1969 Western?

6 | There is a word on the map that, if its last letter was changed, would become the name of a primitive weapon. What is it?

The Knowledge

7 | Which twentieth-century English novelist and poet, whose works include a novel that was banned in Britain for over thirty years, can be found on the map?

8 | Which British director, born in 1936, is known for his films that cover social issues such as homelessness, poverty and workers' rights? His surname can be found on the map.

9 | Which American singer changed her surname from Fowles to a name that can be found on the map? She is best known for her disco anthems.

MAP 46

Sefton Park
Liverpool, England

Park

Located in a district of the same name, Sefton Park is a
large park in the south of Liverpool. The land had been
bought by the council in 1867 to build a green space in
order to improve the health and leisure time of the people of
Liverpool.

The park is designed around a series of circular and oval
footpaths that frame areas of grassland and two water-
courses. The surrounding streets are made up of traditional
Victorian terraces, many of them back-to-back.

Each year Africa Oyé takes place in Sefton Park. It is the
UKs largest festival of African music, is attended by tens of
thousands of people and is entirely free.

QUESTIONS

It's on the Map

1 | How many pavilions ('Pav.') can you find on the map?

2 | Can you identify a road that might be required to power a children's toy?

3 | Can you find a feature that shares its name with a French apple brandy?

Cryptic Challenges

4 | Can you identify three words on the map that can each be anagrammed as one of the following, ignoring the spaces?

       a | Dried ladle
       b | Rangy hair
       c | Old agents

5 | Can you find a path on the map that, if another letter was added in front of it, would become the name for a distinctive men's hairstyle, as well as also the name of a fish?

6 | Can you find a word on the map that sounds like a place for certain aquatic mammals to swim?

The Knowledge

7 | Can you name the writer who created a fictional detective that first appeared in a novel with the title *Knots and Crosses*? There is a feature on the map that bears this writer's surname.

8 | Which footballer, born in Leeds in 1986, has earned over sixty caps for England and yet has a Twitter handle that makes him sound extremely uninteresting? He shares his surname with a road on the map.

9 | Which location on the map is an octagonal Grade-II*-listed Victorian building that contains one of the oldest horticultural collections in Britain?

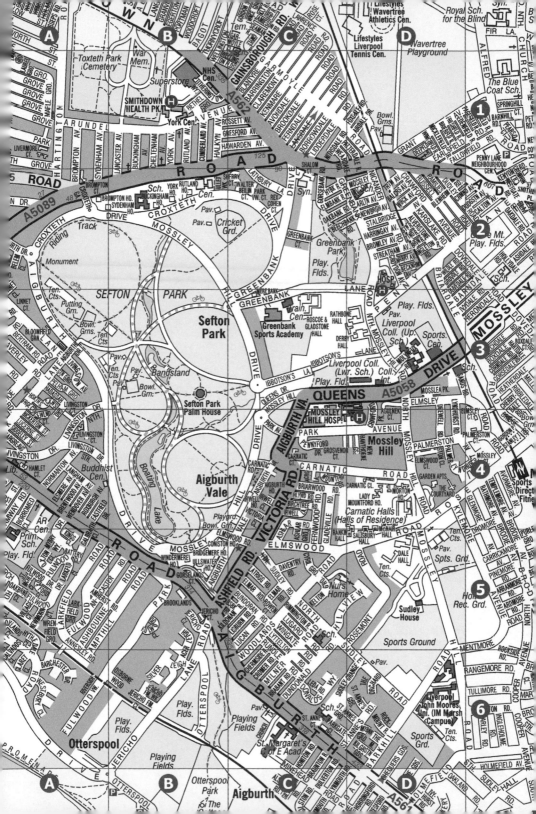

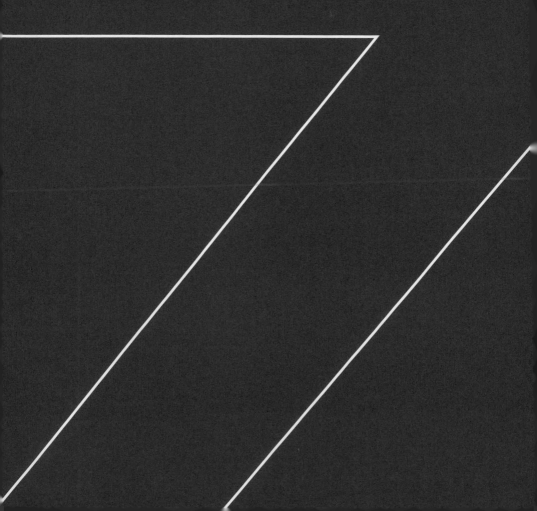

Phyllis Pearsall was awarded a civilian MBE in HM The Queen's birthday honours of 1986, with the investiture on 14th June.

MAP 47

Windermere
Lake District, England

Lake and town

The largest lake in England, Windermere forms a ribbon stretching through the Lake District north of Kendal. Formed by glaciations it is famed for its natural beauty and surrounding hills and dales, and has been a major tourist resort since the arrival of the railway in 1847.

Windermere may describe either the lake or the town of that name. Windermere Town itself is only one of the settlements on the lake's shores, the other major towns being Ambleside and Bowness. The lake itself is relatively young, forming around 16,000 years ago at the end of the last Ice Age. The lake is either ten or eleven miles long, depending on where in the River Leven you consider the lake to end. It contains eighteen islands.

The lake has been the site of numerous water-speed record attempts, as well as the largest open water swim in the UK, and it is the subject of many romantic poems – even featuring in 'There was a Boy' by William Wordsworth.

QUESTIONS

It's on the Map

1 | A touching road and close on the map both share the same name, which is a word that refers to a part of your face. What is it?

2 | Which feature shares its name with a traditional Christmas decoration?

3 | Can you locate a street that shares its name with a prominent feature on a well-known red-and-white national flag?

4 | Which road on the map shares its name with a city in the San Francisco Bay area of California?

Cryptic Challenges

5 | Which word on the map, written backwards, would be a unit of distance?

6 | Can you pinpoint the words on the map that can be anagrammed into the following phrases, ignoring the spaces?

      a | Led big seat
      b | Roster

7 | What road would become the surname of a leading British sitcom actress who died in 2018, if one letter was changed?

The Knowledge

8 | Which location on the map shares its name with a nineteenth-century English priest whose name is used in a term for a type of malapropism?

9 | Which word on the map shares its name with the surname of the person who decorated the dome of St Paul's Cathedral, London?

10 | Can you identify a natural feature on the map that was renamed, after she had climbed it, to share its name with the widow of King William IV?

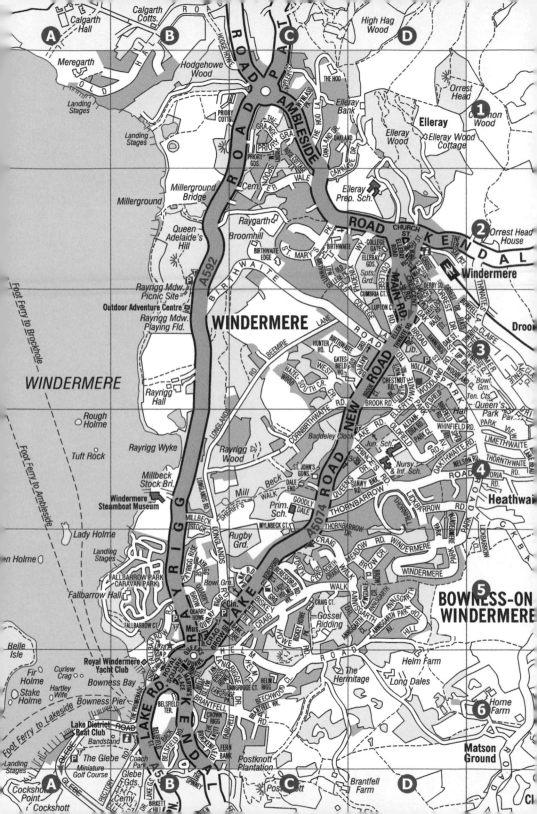

MAP 48

Saltwell Park
Gateshead, England

Park

Known as the People's Park since its opening in 1876, Saltwell Park is a Victorian park in Gateshead, North East England. It was once a stately home and gardens but is now a public park incorporating tennis courts, bowling and putting greens and an artificial boating lake with a wooded island.

Saltwell Towers at the centre of the park is a large Gothic mansion built for the Wailes family in the nineteenth century. But the fast industrialisation of Gateshead, the poor living conditions, contaminated drinking water and ill health of local people soon led the council to purchase the land in order to create a park to help improve the lives of the poor in the area.

Since 1877 there have been animals kept in Saltwell Park, including monkeys and a raccoon. Today the menagerie consists of only a few peafowl, pheasants and rabbits.

QUESTIONS

It's on the Map

1 | Can you find a feature on the map that shares its name with a type of medal awarded at the Olympics?

2 | Which road on the map shares its name with a Mediterranean island?

3 | Can you identify a location that shares its name with the surname of a member of the Beatles?

Cryptic Challenges

4 | Where might you go to play a game of 'checkers'?

5 | Which word on the map sounds like two words that would describe a spoiled drink?

6 | Can you identify a thoroughfare that, if one letter was changed, would denote an island off the coast of France?

The Knowledge

7 | Which location on the map is a Victorian Gothic building that was built by a noted stained glass manufacturer?

8 | Which road on the map shares a name with a noted Welsh rugby union captain, first capped in 2009, who holds the record for most caps gained as Welsh captain?

9 | Which twentieth-century British poet laureate was appointed in 1972, and remained in the role until his death? His surname can be found on the map.

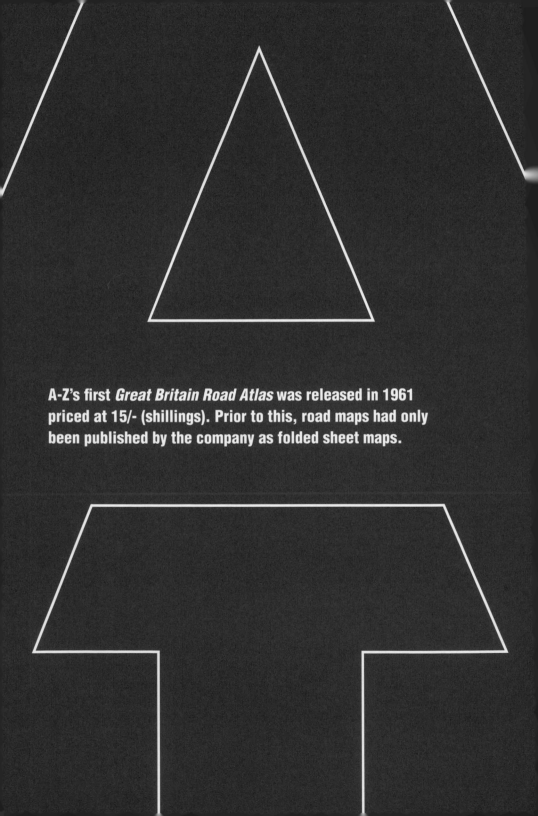

A-Z's first *Great Britain Road Atlas* was released in 1961 priced at 15/- (shillings). Prior to this, road maps had only been published by the company as folded sheet maps.

MAP 49

Town Moor
Newcastle upon Tyne, England

Park

There are not many modern cities in which you can watch cattle grazing by the centre of town, but on Newcastle Town Moor common land rights are still exercised. The moor itself is more than 1,000 acres, making it larger than Hampstead Heath and Hyde Park combined.

The moor has long been a site of political demonstrations in the city, from those opposing the Iraq war and the poll tax, to a demonstration of 200,000 people in 1873 calling for male suffrage.

The moor has seen many sporting events over the years including rabbit coursing and horse racing, and it was also once the site of a smallpox isolation hospital. The last horse race on the moor took place in 1881 and the hospital was demolished in 1958.

QUESTIONS

It's on the Map

1 | Can you find a day of the week on the map?

2 | Locate the Netherlands on the map, if you can. You are looking for its alternative name.

3 | Can you identify a feature on the map that shares its name with a five-letter Welsh county? Beware: it is written in very small writing!

Cryptic Challenges

4 | Can you locate a word that, if it gained an additional final letter, would become the surname of a star-cross'd lover?

5 | Where on the map might you be able to 'compete' against a former Formula One champion?

6 | Can you find a word on the map that, if its second vowel was changed, would become an island in Arthurian legend?

The Knowledge

7 | Which sports venue, that first hosted a game in 1880, contains a stand that is named after a former execution site? It is shown on the map.

8 | Which popular British TV entertainer, who died in 2017, first appeared on stage describing himself as 'The Mighty Atom'? Can you identify a feature on the map that bears his name?

9 | First opened in 1873, which map feature is the oldest park in Newcastle upon Tyne?

MAP 50

Holyrood Park
Edinburgh, Scotland

Royal Park

Holyrood Park on the eastern edge of Edinburgh's Old Town is a Royal Park belonging to Queen Elizabeth II. The park stretches from the foot of The Royal Mile out to the volcanic rocks of King Arthur's Seat. The climb up the crags, or to the top of Arthur's Seat, is popular all year round with tourists and locals. From these vantage points it is possible to look over the tower blocks of the Dumbiedykes up to Edinburgh Castle and across to other landmarks including St Mary's Cathedral, the Balmoral Hotel and Easter Road Stadium.

Just at the edge of the park stand two key buildings of the Scottish State, one is Holyrood Palace, the official residence of the Queen in Edinburgh, and the other is the Scottish Parliament, also called Holyrood. The parliament building itself is a modernist riot of architecture built around the ancient house of the Marquis of Queensbury.

QUESTIONS

It's on the Map

1 | Can you find the name of a racing animal on the map? And can you find the noise it sometimes makes too?

2 | The name of one of the eight planets in the solar system can be found on the map. Which planet is it?

3 | Can you find the name of an ornamental design used for patterning fabric on the map? It occurs several times.

Cryptic Challenges

4 | Can you find a word on the map that, if its second letter was changed, would become a common punctuation symbol?

5 | Which road sounds like an appropriate place to take afternoon tea outdoors?

6 | Which word, found multiple times on the map, can be split up into four parts which could, taken together, mean 'quiet break upon meadow'?

The Knowledge

7 | Which map landmark is an ancient volcano that was once described by the Scottish writer Robert Louis Stevenson as 'a hill for magnitude, a mountain in virtue of its bold design'?

8 | Which Scottish literary figure is commemorated by a monument modelled on the Choragic Monument of Lysicrates in Athens? It is located near the edge of the map area, but is not marked.

9 | In which former royal burgh in Angus did a noted Scottish independence leader destroy its castle, back in 1297? Can you identify a road on the map that shares its name?

BONUS QUIZ

It's on the Map

There are many names that repeat in roads and features in towns and cities across the country, and no doubt you managed to spot some of them as you made your way through the book.

As a final challenge, see if you can find all of the maps that contain the following words. For each word, you will be given the total number of maps that it appears on, and also – to make it easier – the number of maps in each section that it appears in. Note that this is not the number of times the word appears in total, since it may appear multiple times on some maps, but rather the number of distinct maps that it appears on.

Words that are counted in the numbers below will be written without abbreviation, entirely in the coloured area of the map. If the word itself crosses into the yellow area, it is not counted (e.g. the 'Churchill' in square D1 of Map 29, and in square D5 of Map 35, are not counted in the list for 'Churchill' below). None of the words are split over two lines, or run into the centre fold of the book.

WORD	NUMBER TO FIND	HISTORY	SPORT	ENTERTAIN-MENT	TRANSPORT	NATURE
Churchill	6	1	3	1	1	0
Jubilee	6	2	0	1	3	0
Springfield	8	0	3	2	0	3*
Orchard	17	4	3	5	1	4
Victoria	25	5	5	4	5	6

* One of the Springfields in section 5 is written as SPRING FIELD since another road runs through the middle of the text.

SOLUTIONS

ABBREVIATIONS

Av.	Avenue
Cl.	Close
Cotts.	Cottages
Cr./Cres.	Crescent
Ct.	Court
Dr.	Drive
Ga.	Gate
Gds./Gdns./Gs.	Gardens
Gro.	Grove
Ho.	House
La.	Lane
M.	Mews
Pas.	Passage
Pde.	Parade
Pk.	Park
Pl.	Place
Rd.	Road
Rw.	Row
Sq.	Square
St.	Street
T./Ter.	Terrace
Wk./Wlk.	Walk
Wy.	Way
Yd.	Yard

Reminder: Unless specifically stated in the question, answers found in the yellow area of the map are not counted.

MAP 1

1. Catherine Wheel Yd. (C1)
2. Shepherd St. (A1) and White Horse St. (B1)
3. There are 3: White Horse St. (B1), Blue Ball Yd. (C1), Teal St. (D4)
   There is also Greencoat Row (D5)/Greencoat Place (D6–D5), but this is a compound word rather than a single word. You might also include Colour Ct. (D1)
4. Vane St. (D6) – it sounds like 'vain'
5. Angel Ct. (D1) – a court for angels?
6. Stable Yd. (C2)/Stable Yd. Rd. (D2)/Stable Yard Gate (D2) – a 'stable yard' would be an unchanging unit of distance
7. Clarence Ho. (D2) – previously the residence of various royals, including both King William IV and Queen Elizabeth The Queen Mother, it has been the official residence of Charles, Prince of Wales since 2003.
8. Eccleston Pl. (A6)/Eccleston St. (A6)/Eccleston Bridge (B6)/Eccleston Yd. (A6) – Christopher Eccleston was the first actor to play the Doctor who was born after the show first aired in 1963
9. Peabody Estate (D6) – when Marty travels back in time to 1955, he almost immediately crashes straight into a barn on the Peabody Farm.

MAP 2

1. Unicorn [Theatre] (B5)
2. There are 10: B1, C1, D1, A2, C2, C3, 2 in B5, A6, D6
3. There are 10: Royal Mint Street (D2), Royal Mint Pl. (D2), Royal Mint Court (D3), Cardamom Building (D5), Cayenne Ct. (D5–D6), Fennel Apartments (C6–C5), Caraway Apartments (C6–D6), Tamarind Ct. (D6), Ginger Apartments (D6), Coriander Ct. (D6), Cinnamon Wharf (D6) and Saffron Wharf (D6). There is also Vanilla & Sesame Ct. (D6), but these are not usually considered to be herbs or spices
4. Seething Gdns. (B2)/Seething La. (B2)
5. Beehive Pas. (Passage) (A1) – the beehive was a popular hairstyle in the 1960s
6. Four Seasons (B2)
7. Saracens Head Yd. (C1) – the Romans used the term Saracen to describe Arabs from Syria, but the term later became more widely used for any Arab who fought against the Crusaders
8. Curlew Street (C6–D6) – the curlew, whose name is imitative of its characteristic call, can be found worldwide
9. Pepys Street (B2–C2) – Samuel Pepys lived from 1633 to 1703, and his private diary is an important source of information on the English Restoration period

MAP 3

1. The Greenwich Foot Tunnel (B1), which runs beneath the River Thames between Cutty Sark for Maritime Greenwich and Island Gds. DLR stations
2. Deer Park (D3), Hare and Billet Road (C4–C5) and The Squirrels (C6); you might also have thought of Horseshoe Cl. (B1), Horseferry Pl. (B2) or General Wolfe Road (C4), but these are not standalone animal names
3. Circus St. (B3)/Gloucester Circus (B3)/Circus Gate (C3)
4. Bandstand (D3)
5. Maze Hill (D2)
6. Smiles Pl. (B5)
7. Locke's Wharf (A1) – *Locke* was directed by Steven Knight and released in 2013
8. Dacre Pl. (D6) – Paul Dacre was the editor of the *Daily Mail* from 1992 to 2018
9. John Penn St. (A4) – John Penn (1729–1795) was the last governor of colonial Pennsylvania

MAP 4

1. Oakley Rd. (C6)
2. Pleasant Pl. (A6)
3. Baalbec Rd. (A4) – another valid answer would be Napier T. (Terrace) (A6)
4. Myddleton Avenue (B1)
5. Crusoe Mews (C1–D1)
6. Balls Pond Rd. (C5–D5)
7. Wordsworth Rd. (D3–D4) – William Wordsworth (1770–1850) famously wrote 'I Wandered Lonely as a Cloud', also commonly known as 'Daffodils'
8. Oldfield Rd. (D2) – Mike Oldfield is an English multi-instrumentalist whose *Tubular Bells* was used in the 1973 film *The Exorcist*
9. Arundel Gro. (D4) – Arundel Castle in Sussex is the seat of the Duke of Norfolk

MAP 5

1. Rook Island (B1) and Cranbrook Castle Tennis Club (D1) – castle and rook in chess are both different names for the same piece
2. There are 18 places of worship marked with a cross: D1, A3, B3, C3, C4, A5, B5, C5, four in D5, and two each in B6, C6 and D6. There is also a 19th one (A5) at the far right edge of the map, which might be tricky to spot
3. Merlin Rd. (B3) – Merlin is a wizard from Arthurian legend
4. Seventh Av. (D5) – 'seventh heaven' is a term for eternal bliss, as is nirvana
5. Comet Cl. (B5) – on the map, the 'Cl.' needs to be expanded to 'Close', i.e. a word meaning nearby
6. Belgrave Road (D2) – the word 'grave' can be found within 'Belgrave'
7. Toronto Av. (D5) – Toronto is the capital of Ontario, and has a population of around 2.7 million people
8. The Chase (B5) – one of the show's 'Chasers' is Shaun Wallace, also known as 'The Dark Destroyer'
9. Arran Dr. (B2–B3) – Arran, also known as the Isle of Arran, lies in the Firth of Clyde off the southwest coast of Scotland, and is also the seventh-largest island in all of Scotland

MAP 6

1. There are 3 disabled toilets (B1, B6, C2), and 5 car parks (A2/A3, A4, B1, B2, B3, B6)
2. Chestnut Avenue (B1/B2/B3) – it is labelled as being open from 7.30am to 7.00pm
3. Summer Road (A5), at its westernmost end
4. Cigarette Island Park (A4–B4)
5. Lime Walk (B3/B4)
6. Ferry Rd. (D6)
7. Aragon Av. (B5) – Catherine of Aragon was Queen of England from 1509 to 1533
8. The Island (C6) – this dystopian science fiction film centralises around the concept of human cloning and organ harvesting
9. Boyle Farm Island (C6)/Boyle Farm Rd. (C6) – Robert Boyle first published the law that bears his name in 1662

MAP 7

1. Wellington Sq. (B4/B5)
2. Adventure: Smugglers Adventure (C4) and Adventure Golf (C5)
3. There are 8: [Blacklands] Primary School (A2), Elphinstone Primary School (B2/C2), Hastings College (C2), [Castledown Primary] School (D3), [Sacred Heart RC Primary] School (D3), Torfield School (D3), [East Sussex] College (B4), University [of Brighton] (B5)
4. Waterworks Rd. (B3/B4)
5. Broomgrove (C2/D2)
6. Sturdee Place (C5), which sounds like a 'sturdy place'
7. The Bourne Old (D4–D3) – 'Bourne' occurs in *The Bourne Identity*, *The Bourne Supremacy*, *The Bourne Ultimatum*, *The Bourne Legacy* and *Jason Bourne*
8. Redmayne Dr. (A5) – Eddie Redmayne won the academy award for best actor for his portrayal of renowned theoretical physicist Stephen Hawking
9. Denmark Place (B5) – Sweyn Forkbeard was King of Denmark from 986 to 1014

MAP 8

1. There are 4: C1, A6, B6, D6
2. B2 – on the corner of Round Church Street and Bridge Street
3. Rose Crescent (B3)
4. Christ's Pieces (D3)
5. Garret Hostel La. (A3) – a garret is a top-floor or attic room
6. Hyde Park Corner (D6) – at Hyde Park Speakers' Corner in London, speakers gather and talk on many subjects
7. Bridge of Sighs (A2) – built in 1831, much later than the Bridge of Sighs in Venice, Cambridge's similarly named crossing connects parts of St John's College together
8. Portugal St. (B1/B2) – Portugal joined the European Union on 1 January 1986
9. Downing Street (C5) – these are names of the Chief Mousers to the Cabinet Office, or in other words the cats that have lived at 10 Downing Street

MAP 9

1. Warren Drive (B5), The Warren (D5) and The Warren (C6)
2. The orange-coloured buildings on the join of A2 to B2
3. Cwmwbwb (B6)
4. Maxton Court (C3) – 'Max ton'
5. Trap Well (D1)
6. Van Farm (D4)
7. Snowden Court (C3) – Edward Snowden leaked highly classified information from the NSA
8. Tommy Cooper Statue (B4) – Tommy Cooper was a highly successful magician, despite pretending to be otherwise
9. King Edward Avenue (B4) – King Edward I claimed various rights over Scotland, which led to war

MAP 10

1. There are 3: B1, D5, A6
2. Floral Clock (C2) – this is a clock, made out of plants, that actually tells the correct time
3. Heriot Cross (C4) – the building is both cross-shaped and contains the word 'cross' in its name
4. Simpson Loan (C6/D6)
5. Riddle's Ct. (D3)
6. The Royal Scots Dragoon Guards Museum (B4) – once you change the double 'o' to a single 'o', you reveal a dragon
7. Nightingale Way (C6) – Florence Nightingale (1820–1910), also known as 'the Lady with the Lamp', due to her work in hospitals during the Crimean War
8. Dunlop's Ct. (C4) – Dunlop Sports is a well-known brand of sporting goods, and Dunlop Rubber/Dunlop Tyres are well-known for their vehicle tyres
9. Earl Grey St. (A5/A6) – Earl Grey tea is thought to have been named after Charles Grey, the 2nd Earl Grey (1764–1845), who was prime minister when slavery was abolished in the British Empire

MAP 11

1. Forty Avenue (B2–C1)/Forty Cl. (B2)/Forty Lane (D1)
2. Dorothy: Dorothy Av. (A6)
3. Talisman: Talisman Way (B2)
4. Barn Rise (C1)
5. SSE Arena (C3) – SSE stands for south-south-east, which lies at the 157.5 degree point on a compass face
6. The Crossways (C1/D1)
7. Sylvia Plath: Sylvia Gs. (Gardens) (D6)
8. Farnborough Close (D1), marked on the map as 'Farnbgh Cl.' – the Farnborough Air Show takes place every other year, and alternates with the Paris Air show
9. Pendolino Wy. (C6) – Pendolino trains are used in countries such as Italy, Spain, Poland, Portugal, Slovenia, Finland and the United Kingdom

MAP 12

1. Autumn St. (A5) – there is also a Springwood Close (A6) in the map area, but it is not a single word and is abbreviated to 'Spgwd Cl'
2. Celebration Avenue (C2)
3. Pudding Mill Lane (B6)
4. Knights Bridge (B2)
5. Bingo (D5) – somewhere to go if you're feeling lucky, and it sounds like 'bin go'
6. Biggerstaff Rd. (C5) – it sounds like 'bigger staff'
7. It was built for the 2012 Summer Olympics, and it was formerly known as the Olympic Stadium
8. Carpenters Road (A3–C4) – Karen and Richard Carpenter, jointly known as The Carpenters, recorded ten albums over their fourteen-year career
9. Hitchcock Lane (C3) – Alfred Hitchcock (1899–1980) directed over fifty feature films

MAP 13

1. Centre Court (C6) – it is the name of a Wimbledon shopping centre
2. Dairy Walk (B4)
3. The school building in C1 is in the shape of a 'J'
4. Winterfold Cl. (B2) – it sounds like 'winter' and 'fold', and origami involves a lot of folding
5. The gap: Gap Road (D5) – as in 'mind the gap', which is announced on certain platforms where there is a particularly large gap between the train and the platform. These platforms include the Central line platforms at Bank, and the Bakerloo line platforms at Piccadilly Circus
6. Seymour Road (A3) – 'see more road'
7. 77 years. Fred Perry (1909–1995) was the last British tennis player to win that title, back in 1936
8. South Park Gardens (D6) – *South Park* is a US show for Comedy Central
9. Augustus Road (A1–C1) – Augustus (63 BC–14 AD) was the first emperor of the Roman Empire.

MAP 14

1. There are 10: Spring Mews (A1), Hansom Mews (B1), Cumberland Mews (D2), Silk Mews (D2), Whitacre Mews (D2), Percival Mews (A3), Meadow Mews (A4), Paragon Mews (A4), Usborne Mews (B5), Pickle Mews (C5).
2. South Island Place (B6–C6) – North Island and South Island form most of the land mass of New Zealand
3. Cleaver Street/Cleaver Square (D1–D2)
4. Jupiter Ct. (C6) – these are the initials of the planets working in order towards the sun
5. Bland Ho. (B1)
6. Windmill Row (C2)
7. Juno Ct. (C6) – *Juno* won an Oscar for best original screenplay
8. 20.16 metres (22 yards)
9. Graphite Sq. (A1) – when graphite was first used to create writing tools, it was incorrectly thought to be a form of lead. The name stuck, even though it is inaccurate

MAP 15

1. There are 5: A3, B3, D3, A6/B6 and D6
2. Capel Ct. (D4)
3. Walnut Cl. (A4) and The Chestnuts (A3)
4. Watershoot Cl. (C3) – it sounds like 'water chute', which is another term for a water slide
5. Kinder Ho. (D4)
6. Star Ct. (B6)
7. Burma Av. (D6) – the name was changed in an attempt to remove former colonial spellings of the country's name
8. Somme Rd. (D6) – the Battle of the Somme took place between the 1st July and 18th November 1916
9. Park La. (D2) – Park Lane costs £350 to buy, second only to Mayfair at £400

MAP 16

1. The school in C3 forms a perfect upside-down 'E' shape
2. A red dot – the war memorial is in C5
3. The library and museum in B4, plus the empty map area between them
4. The Big Apple (C1) – 'the Big Apple' is often used to refer to New York City
5. At the Recreation Ground (found separately in A2, A5, C5, B6) – since 'ground' can mean 'pulverized'
6. Oxford Street and Cambridge Street (D4–D3) form 'Cambridge' and 'Oxford' in narrow parallel shapes, just like at the start of the yearly Oxford-Cambridge Boat Race on the Thames
7. Drury Lane (B4) – The Muffin Man's author is not known, but the first recorded publication of its words was around 1820
8. Bell Rd. (C2) – Alexander Graham Bell (1847–1922) is also known for his work on metal detectors, hydrofoils and the design of early aeroplanes
9. Rugby School (B5) – rugby is said to have been developed at Rugby School during the early 19th century

MAP 17

1. Paddock Cl. (D5)
2. Bowler Wy. (D2)
3. Hermitage Road (A5–B3)
4. Nursery End (C6)
5. The Haven (C1/D1)
6. Pocket End (C6/D6) – the hole on a pool table is known as a 'pocket'
7. Coe Av. (A1) – Sebastian Coe also won two Olympic golds in the 1500 metres
8. Chichester Cl. (B6) – Sir Francis Chichester sailed from Plymouth in August 1966 and, after a stop in Sydney, returned after 226 days of sailing in May 1967
9. Paula Radcliffe Athletics Stadium (C3/D3) – Paula Radcliffe won the London Marathon in 2002, 2003 and 2005, and the New York Marathon in 2004, 2007 and 2008

MAP 18

1. Hope St. (D5); Love La. (D3)
2. Century Ct. (A5)
3. Firing Line (B2)
4. Barrack La. (D3) – it can be split to form 'bar rack'
5. Great Western La. (C4-C5) – a great Western, since John Wayne was renowned for his starring roles in Westerns, and appeared in 83 of them during his career
6. Dray Ct. (C4) – it is literally 'yard', written backwards
7. Saunders Rd. (C5) – Jennifer Saunders appeared in 'French and Saunders' along with Dawn French
8. Tredegar St. (D4) – Tredegar was the birthplace of Aneurin Bevan, who was Minister of Health at the founding of the National Health Service in 1948
9. Morgan Arcade (C4)/David Morgan Apts. (C4) – Cliff Morgan earned 29 caps between 1951 and 1958, and later became a presenter, commentator, programme maker and a BBC executive

MAP 19

1. Macbeth St. (D4)/Macbeth Pl. (D4)
2. Baltic Pl. (A4)/Baltic St. (A4-A5)/Baltic Ct.(A5) - the Baltic Sea is to the east of Sweden
3. Brookside St. (A3) – Brookside aired for 21 years
4. Holywell St. (B3) – it sounds like 'holy well'
5. Burgher St. (C3–D3) – it is pronounced like 'burger'
6. Nuneaton Street (A5–B4) – it sounds like 'none eaten'
7. Law St. (B3) – Jude Law was Oscar nominated in 1999 for his role in *The Talented Mr Ripley*
8. Garfield St. (A2) – Garfield, the lazy orange cat, was apparently named after his creator's grandfather, James A. Garfield Davis, who was in turn named after US President James A. Garfield
9. Troon St. (B5) – The Royal Troon Golf Club in South Ayrshire first hosted the Open in 1962. In 2016 the tournament was won by Henrik Stenson

MAP 20

1. B3 – with 4 car parks
2. Hospital (B6), police station (C3), fire station (B5)
3. There are 8 (although 3 are parallel to roads and hard to see): C2, 4 in C3, D3, B4, C4. There is also St Andrew's Cathedral in D3, but it does not have a cross
4. The Scores (C2–D3)/East Scores (D3) – a score is a group of twenty
5. The Links (B2) – it sounds like 'the lynx'
6. Largo Road (A6–C4) – 'largo' is a musical term meaning 'slow and dignified'
7. Hamilton Av. (C5) – *Hamilton* won 11 Tony awards, 1 Grammy and 8 Olivier
8. Thistle La. (C3/C4) – the thistle has been the national emblem of Scotland since the 13th century
9. Watson Avenue (C4) – Tom Watson (actually Thomas Watson) also won the US Open, and the Open Championship 5 times

MAP 21

1. Upper Brook Street (A4)/Brook Street (B4–D3); there is also Brook's M. (Mews) (C4)
2. Carpenter St. (C5)
3. Saddle Yd. (C6)
4. Three Kings Yd. (C4) – the Magi were the Biblical kings who visited Jesus in the manger. There are often said to have been three, but this count does not appear in the Bible, and indeed they are mentioned in only one of the four gospels.
5. Haunch of Venison Yd. (C3) – venison is deer meat
6. Wigmore Street (A3–C2)/Wigmore Pl. (C2)/Wigmore Hall (C2) – it sounds like 'wig more', and a toupee is a small wig
7. D. H. Evans/House of Fraser – the Oxford Street store, previously known as D. H. Evans and more recently as House of Fraser, opened in 1937. It was noted on opening for its escalator hall that rose the full height of the building, which was particularly notable since it was the tallest store on Oxford Street
8. Jason Ct. (B2) – David Jason is particularly noted for his role as Derek 'Del Boy' Trotter in *Only Fools And Horses*
9. Broadbent Street (C4) – Jim Broadbent won the Best Supporting Oscar for *Iris* in 2001

MAP 22

1. Reminder La. (D4)
2. Amsterdam Rd. (A5) – Amsterdam is the capital of the Netherlands
3. Sextant Av. (B6) – a sextant is an instrument used for measuring angular distances
4. Bowman Av. (D2) – it sounds like 'bow man'
5. Findhorn St. (A1) – it sounds like 'find horn'
6. Primrose Wharf (B5) – it sounds like a 'prim rose'
7. Hoy St. (D1) – Sir Chris (Christopher) Hoy was voted 2008 BBC Sports Personality of the Year, and was awarded a knighthood in the 2009 New Year Honours List. He retired from competitive cycling in 2013
8. Rembrandt Cl. (B5) – Rembrandt van Rijn (1606–1669) is widely considered one of the greatest painters of all time
9. Bon Jovi - they performed at The O_2 Arena on 24 June 2007

MAP 23

1. Strand (C4–D4); there is also Strand La. (D4), although it is not a major street
2. Emerald St. (D2)
3. Sardinia St. (D3) – Sardinia has a population of around 1.5 million, and in Italian is known as Sardegna
4. Shorts Gs. (Gardens) (C3)
5. Sandland St. (D2) – it sounds like 'sand land'
6. Broadwick St. (A4–B3) – it could be heard as 'broad wick'
7. Charing Cross Rd. (B3–B4) – the film was *84 Charing Cross Road*, based on a memoir by US writer Helene Hanff
8. Dombey St. (D2) – the novel is *Dombey and Son*, which first appeared in monthly parts from 1 October 1846 to 1 April 1848
9. Nassau St. (A2) – Nassau is the capital of the Bahamas. It is named after the town of Nassau in Germany

MAP 24

1. Paddington St. (C6) – Paddington Bear, created by Michael Bond, is a fictional character in children's literature
2. Homer St. and Homer Rw. (A6)
3. Broad, early and haven: Broad Walk (C2–D5), Early M. (Mews) (D2) and Haven St. (D1)
4. The Hub (B3)
5. Mansfield St. (D6) – it sounds like 'man's field'; Mansfield Mews (D6) is also marked, but is abbreviated to 'Mfld M.'
6. Dumpton Pl. (C1) – it could be heard as 'dump ton'
7. Guy the gorilla. He was a major attraction at the zoo between 1947 and 1978
8. Nash St. (D4) – John Nash created the master plan for the area around Regent's Park, although he did not design all the buildings himself
9. The Incredible Hulk – his waxwork is 4.5 m (14.8 ft) tall, with eyes the size of cricket balls. It was so big it had to be lifted in through the roof

MAP 25

1. Rugby Lodge (C4/C5)
2. Comet Cl. (D3)
3. Jordan Cl. (D4) and Lebanon Cl. (B5)
4. Strangeways (C5) – it sounds like 'strange ways'
5. The Fairway (B1–C1) – it sounds like 'the fair way'
6. Greenbank Road (B5–C5) – it can be read as 'green bank'
7. Hercules Wy. (D3) – Hercules, whose Greek equivalent was Heracles, was noted for his strength, including completing his 12 labours; it is also the middle name of Sir Elton John
8. Robbie Coltrane – he was nominated for a BAFTA for Best Actor in a Supporting Role for the first film in the series, *Harry Potter and the Philosopher's Stone*
9. Whittle Cl. (D3) – Sir Frank Whittle (1907–1996) was an English aviation engineer and pilot who invented the jet engine – he first put forward his vision of jet propulsion in 1928 in his thesis at RAF College, taking out a patent in 1930. A plane using his jet engine had its maiden flight in 1941

MAP 26

1. Sheep St. (C3) and Bull St. (B4–C3); there is also Cowslip Rd. (D5), but a cowslip is a flower
2. Wharf Rd. (B1), Riverbank Gds. (D3) and Marina (D3)
3. Sequoia M. (Mews) (D3) – Sequoia National Park is noted for its huge sequoia trees
4. Holly Orchard (C1)
5. Clopton Ct. (B2)/Clopton Road (B2–B1) – if you change the first vowel in Clopton to 'a', you have the surname of Eric Clapton, the noted rock guitarist
6. Payton St. (C2) – it sounds like 'pay ton'
7. The Gower Memorial (C3) – it was designed by Sir Ronald Gower, and features Shakespeare surrounded by the statues of Hamlet, Lady Macbeth, Prince Hal and Falstaff. Each represents a different element of his work: philosophy, tragedy, history and comedy
8. Springfield Cl. (D6)/Springfield Cottages (D6) – Springfield is the fictional location of The Simpsons, and the state capital of Illinois
9. Cherry Orchard (A4–B4) – *The Cherry Orchard* is the title of a play written by Anton Chekhov, often described as perversely both a tragedy and a comedy

MAP 27

1. Drum Av. (A3)
2. Cinnamon La. (D5)
3. Fawn Cl. (A5) and Stag Wy. (A4)
4. Chalice Hill Cl. (C4), Chalice Pk. (B4) and Chalice Wy. (C5–D5)
5. Launder Close (C4) – money-laundering often involves transfers via foreign banks or businesses
6. Silver St. (C4) – silver has atomic number 47
7. Pendragon Pk. (B3) – Uther Pendragon was the father of King Arthur, according to Geoffrey of Monmouth
8. Avalon Estate (C1) – Avalon is a legendary island, as well as the title of the eighth studio album by Roxy Music, released in 1982
9. Pike Close (A4–A3) – Rosamund Pike starred in *Gone Girl*, directed by David Fincher. She was nominated for Best Actress for both the Oscars and the BAFTAs for the role

MAP 28

1. Well Lane (C6)
2. Heath Road (B4–C3) and Heath T. (Terrace) (C3)
3. The name appears 7 times: Newton M. (Mews) (D5), Newton Lane (written in both D5 and D6), Newton (D6), Newton Hall Dr. (D6), Newton Hall Ct. (D6) and Newton House (D6),
4. Entrance (B2/C2) – if read as a verb, this is the meaning of 'entrance'
5. Bank Cl. (C6)
6. Halton Road (D5) – it sounds like 'halt on road'
7. Tintern Av. (D5) – Tintern Abbey fell into ruin after the dissolution of the monasteries in the 16th century
8. Horrocks Rd. (C6) – Jane Horrocks starred in *Sunshine on Leith*, a musical film set to the music of the Proclaimers, and based on a jukebox musical of the same name
9. Elephant – Jubilee was an Asian elephant, and the first of its kind to be born at the zoo

MAP 29

1. Lord St. (B1), Duke St. (B6) and Baron Rd. (C6)
2. Clinton Av. (C3)
3. Condor Grove (D4–D5)
4. Topping St. (B2)
5. Princess Pde. (Parade) (B1); there are also Princess Ct. (B4) and Princess St. (B4–C4), although these do not fit the clue so well
6. Boardman Av. (D5) – it sounds like 'board man'
7. Blackpool Tower (A3/B3) – an iconic tourist attraction, at 158 m (518 ft) tall it is just under half the height of the 324-m (1,063-ft) Eiffel Tower
8. Gainsborough Rd. (D3) – *The Blue Boy* is perhaps Thomas Gainsborough's (1727–88) best-known work
9. Winter Gardens (B2) – today a Grade II* listed building, it contains a theatre, ballroom and other facilities

MAP 30

1. There are 8: A2, C2, A3, 2 in A5, B5, B6, D6, although the one in A3 may be hidden in the fold of the book
2. Derby Street (D4–D3)
3. Clyde Auditorium (Armadillo) (C6) – armadillos are native to Central and South America
4. Hastie St. (B3) – it can be split into 'has tie'
5. Bunhouse Road (A2–B2) – it sounds like 'bun house'
6. Congress Way (D6)/Congress Road (C6) – the United States Congress is the legislature of the US federal government, and consists of the House, led by its Speaker, and the Senate
7. Fitzroy Lane (D4) – Fitzroy is a shipping forecast area off the northwest coast of Spain, named after Admiral Robert Fitzroy, captain of HMS *Beagle* and the founder of the Met Office in 1854
8. Salvador Dalí – it is a painting Dalí made in 1951 and depicts Jesus Christ from a high angle on the cross in a darkened sky floating over a body of water with boat and fishermen. There are no nails, blood or crown of thorns even though it depicts the crucifixion
9. Palmerston Pl. (C4) – Henry John Temple, 3rd Viscount Palmerston, was British prime minister from 1855–1858 and from 1859–1865

MAP 31

1. Cloud Wy. (D3); Contrail Wy. (C3–D3) – a contrail is the vapour trail left behind by an aircraft
2. Crane, condor and nene: Crane Rd. (C6), Condor Way (C3–D3) and Nene Rd. (D1) - Nene is another name for the Hawaiian Goose
3. Cosmopolitan Wy. (D3), from which the letter 'i' has been left out – a cosmopolitan is a cocktail made with vodka, triple sec, cranberry and lime juice
4. Courtney Rd. (C2C3)/Courtney Wy. (C2) – 'Courtney' sounds like 'caught knee'
5. Chipstead Rd. (C3) – starts with 'chips'
6. Scylla Rd. (D6) – Scylla is a mythological sea monster that devoured sailors
7. Stranraer Wy. (A6) – Stranraer is a town in Dumfries and Galloway that lies at the head of Loch Ryan. An official ferry link to Belfast was established in 1862
8. Scylla Rd. (D6) – Scylla was a monster in Greek mythology that lived on one side of a narrow channel of water opposite her counterpart Charybdis, the personification of a whirlpool – Odysseus had to encounter them during his travels in Homer's Odyssey
9. Terminal 5 – it had 31.9 million passengers on 213,179 flights. This exceeds by some margin the 16.5 million passengers on 118,425 flights for Terminal 2, the 17.7 million passengers on 91,327 flights for Terminal 3, and the 9.5 million passengers on 48,137 flights for Terminal 4. Terminal 1 closed in 2015

MAP 32

1. Pear Pl. (C4)
2. Windmill Wlk. (D3–D4)
3. Mead Rw. (C6)
4. Brad Street (D3) – if its central letters 'a' and 'r' are switched, it forms the word 'Bard'
5. Greenham Cl. (C5–D5) – it can be parsed as 'green' (mouldy) 'ham'
6. Broadwall (D2) – it sounds like 'broad wall'
7. Cleopatra's Needle (A2) is an Egyptian obelisk that was brought to London from Alexandria, Egypt, as a gift to commemorate the British victory over Napoleon at the Battle of the Nile. There are similar obelisks in Paris and New York
8. Holmes T. (Terrace) (C4) – Sherlock Holmes was the detective created by Sir Arthur Conan Doyle. He first appeared in the novel *A Study in Scarlet*
9. Waterloo Station has 24 platforms, although only 22 are in use at the time of writing

MAP 33

1. Tiger Ho. (C5)
2. Stable Street (D1–D2)
3. Polygon [Road] (B3) and The Magic Circle (A6)
4. Speedy Pl. (D5)
5. Lancing St. (B5), which is just south of Doric Way (B4) – lancing takes place during medieval jousting, and Doric is a classical style of architecture
6. Shaw [Theatre] (C5)/Monica Shaw Ct. (C3) – Shaw is a homophone of 'shore'
7. Phoenix Ct. (C3) and Phoenix Road (B4–C3) – Phoenix is the state capital of Arizona, and in mythology a bird that can be reborn out of its own ashes
8. Handel Street (D6) – George Frederick Handel was a German, later British, baroque composer whose works include *Water Music*, a series of orchestral movements designed for a concert for King George I on the River Thames
9. Stephenson Way (A6–A5) – George Stephenson (1781–1848) was appointed as engineer for the construction of the Stockton and Darlington Railway that opened in 1825. It was the first public railway

MAP 34

1. Fountain Sq. (B4)
2. Cardinal: Cardinal Pl. (C2)/Cardinal Walk (C3–C2)
3. Birdcage [Walk] (C1–D1)
4. The Forecourt (C1) – the forecourt is the area outside a petrol station
5. Greencoat Row(D3)/Greencoat Place (D4) – 'green' (environmentally friendly) 'coat'
6. Terminus Pl. (B3) – 'term' 'in' 'US'
7. Hobart Pl. (A2) – Hobart is the state capital of Tasmania. It was named after Robert Hobart, fourth earl of Buckinghamshire, who was secretary of state for the colonies
8. Spenser St. (D2) – Edmund Spenser (1552-1599) was an English poet best known for his long allegorical poem *The Faerie Queene*, celebrating Elizabeth I. It was first published in 1590
9. Mansion House on the Circle and District line, and South Ealing on the Heathrow branch of the Piccadilly line

MAP 35

1. Pounds T. (Terrace) (B3), Penny St. (B6–C6) and Farthing La. (B6). (There is also John Pounds Centre within the map area, but it is not marked on the map.)
2. Centurion Ct. (B5)
3. Tiger Road (A2); and Lion Road (A2–A3), Lion St. (C4) and Lion T. (Terrace) (C4)
4. Short Row (B3)
5. Cascades Centre (D3)
6. The Retreat (D6)
7. Mary Rose Museum (A3) is dedicated to the *Mary Rose*. It served the monarch for 34 years in wars against Scotland and France, before it sank in the English Channel in 1545. After numerous attempts to salvage it over the years, it was finally recovered from the seafloor in 1982
8. Edgbaston Ho. (D5) – Edgbaston in Birmingham is the home cricket ground of Warwickshire County Cricket Club – it held the first test in the 2018 series against India
9. Bilbao and Santander - these Spanish cities on the country's north coast are directly accessible by ferry from Portsmouth

MAP 36

1. Queen Elizabeth Rd. (D3) and Prince of Wales Roundabout (B5) (written 'Prnce of Wls R'bt. on the map). There is also Elizabeth Street (B5-B6)
2. Dolphin Passage (C4) (written as 'Dolphn Ps.' on the map)
3. Constables Rd. (C2–C3)
4. Cowgate Hill (B4)
5. Selbourne Ter. (A4) – if the first letter is changed to 'M' it becomes Melbourne, the capital of Victoria
6. Deal [Road] (C2–D2–D1), which is written in large writing – and a deal is a bargain
7. Bleriot Memorial (D2) – it is dedicated to Louis Bleriot (1872–1936), the pioneering French aviator who became the first person to cross the English Channel in an aeroplane
8. Millais Rd. (A2) – Sir John Everett Millais (1829–96). One of his most famous works is *Ophelia*, painted in 1851–2, showing the character from *Hamlet*
9. Danes Ct. (B1) – Claire Danes plays the role of Carrie Mathison, a CIA operative, in *Homeland*, for which she has won multiple Emmy and Golden Globe awards

MAP 37

1. Swallow St. (A4)
2. Beak St. (B4)
3. Florence St. (A6)
4. Needless Alley (B3)
5. Ladywell Walk (C5)
6. Minories (C2) – you can add 'it' to form 'minorities'
7. Chamberlain Sq. (A3) is named in honour of Joseph Chamberlain (1836–1914), mayor of Birmingham in the latter half of the 19th century. His son Neville was British prime minister at the outbreak of the Second World War, but was replaced by Winston Churchill in 1940
8. Hurst Street (C5–D6) – Geoff Hurst scored a hat-trick in England's 1966 World Cup final, helping them to win 4-2. He remains the only player to have scored three goals in a World Cup final, and was knighted in 1998
9. Snow Hill (B1), Moor Street (D3) and New Street (B4)

MAP 38

1. Pound La. (D1)
2. Clover Avenue (A3), Harebell Walk (A3–A2), Bluebell Drive/Bluebell Recreation Ground (A3–B3) and Woodbine Walk (A3) – a woodbine is a type of honeysuckle
3. Blair Gro. (A4) and Eden Gr. (A4) – Tony Blair was British prime minister from 1997 to 2007 and Anthony Eden from 1955 to 1957
4. Foxland Cl. (A3) – vulpine means 'relating to foxes'
5. Picton Cft. (Croft) (A3) – if the third letter 'c' is changed to 's', it forms the word 'piston'
6. Quartz Point (D6) – quartz is a mineral, and a point is sharp
7. Trident Ct. (B5) – a trident is the weapon wielded by Aquaman, and one of the seven Relics of Atlantis
8. Drake Cft. (Croft) (A1) – Sir Francis Drake (1540–1596) was an English sea captain and explorer who carried out the second circumnavigation of the world in a single expedition. Pelican was later renamed the *Golden Hind*, and *Benedict* was later forcibly traded for Christopher. He also acquired a sixth ship shortly after setting out, the *Santa Maria*, which was itself renamed to *Mary*
9. Birmingham International Airport – the first section of the M42 was opened in November 1976, linking the airport to the M6 motorway

MAP 39

1. Mulberry St. (B2)
2. Lyceum Theatre (B3) – there is also a Lyceum Theatre in the West End of London
3. Rhodes St. (D3)
4. a) Waingate (B1); b) Mortimer St. (B5); c) Esperanto Pl. (B2)
5. Lenton St. (B6) – if the fourth letter 't' was changed to an 'n', it would form the surname of John Lennon
6. Paternoster Rw. (B4) – the paternoster is the Lord's Prayer, and a row is an argument
7. The Crucible Theatre (B2) – since 1977 it has been the venue for the Snooker World Championship
8. Cheney Row (A3) – Dick Cheney was the 46th vice-president of the United States, serving under George W Bush from 2001 to 2009. He was a member of the US House of Representatives for a district in Wyoming from 1978 to 1989
9. Blue, purple, yellow and black

MAP 40

1. Pigeon St. (D1), Mallard St. (C2–C3), Rockdove A. (Avenue) (B3), Heron St. (A5), Falcon Ct. (A5) and Peregrine St. (B5). (There is also a fictional bird in the map area, with Phoenix Street (C1), but it is written on the map as 'Phnx St.')
2. Trumpet St. (B2). (There is also Bugle Street (A2–A3) in the map area, but it appears in abbreviated form as 'Bgl S.')
3. Asia Ho. (C2) adjoins India Ho. (C2)
4. Playfair St. (D6) – 'play fair'
5. Cross St. (B1)
6. New York St. (C1)
7. Whitworth Art Gallery (D6) – it was founded by Robert Darbishire with a donation from Sir Joseph Whitworth, an engineer, inventor and philanthropist
8. Bale St. (B2) – Gareth Bale is a Welsh footballer who moved from Tottenham Hotspur to Real Madrid for just over 100 million euros in 2013
9. Harold Macmillan. The station was renamed Manchester Piccadilly on 12th September 1960, replacing the previous name of Manchester London Road that had been used since the first half of the 19th century

MAP 41

1. Spring St. (A2) and Spring M. (Mews) (C1)
2. Archery Cl. (B2)
3. Basil St. (C6–C5)
4. Pont St. (C6) – if you change the vowel 'o' to 'i', it forms the word 'pint'
5. Easleys M. (Mews) (D2) – if 'W' is inserted at the front, it forms 'Weasleys'. The Weasleys are one of the central families in the *Harry Potter* novels and films, and Ron Weasley is one of the three main characters
6. Homer Rw./Homer St. (B1) – Homer is a Greek epic poet, and if the middle letter 'm' is changed to 'v', it becomes the word 'hover'
7. Apsley House (D5) – it was the London townhouse of the Duke of Wellington. Now open to the public as a museum and art gallery, it is sometimes known as the Wellington Museum. It was at one time called 'Number 1 London' as it was the first house passed by visitors after the former toll gates at Knightsbridge
8. Joy of Life Fountain (C4–D4) – it was installed in 1963 from a design by Thomas Huxley-Jones, and also features four bronze children emerging from the water's edges
9. Reeves M. (Mews) (D3) – George Reeves (1914–59) was noted for his portrayal of Superman in the 1950s US TV series, *Adventures of Superman*. Without its final letter, 's', it can also refer to Christopher Reeve, who played Superman in a series of films from 1978 onwards

MAP 42

1. Goat Wharf (B2)
2. Maze Rd. (D3)
3. Romulus Ct. (A3) – his brother was Remus
4. Defoe Av. (D3) – the author was Daniel Defoe
5. Haining Cl. (D1) – if you change the first letter from 'h' to 'r', it forms the word 'raining'
6. Hearne Rd. (D2) – if the letter 'n' is changed to 's', it forms the word 'hearse', the specially constructed car that carries the coffin at a funeral
7. a) Lion Gate (C6, in Lion Gate Gardens) – 'tail gone' is an anagram ('agitated') of the answer, and a lion gate would be a 'beast container' (i.e. something that contains a beast) b) Visitor Centre (C4) – 'five' is V, and then 'is it or' followed by 'cent' (a fraction of a dollar) and 're' (with respect to), giving an amenity
8. Queen Charlotte's Cottage (A5/B5) – it was a rustic cottage for Queen Charlotte, wife of King George III, intended as a retreat rather than a residence.
9. Harvey Ho. (B1) – PJ Harvey has won the Mercury Prize twice, first in 2001 for her album *Stories from the City, Stories from the Sea* and again in 2011 for her album *Let England Shake*
10. Davies Alpine House (C3) – opened in 2006, it shows at any one time around 200 of Kew's world-renowned collection of over 7,000 alpine plants

MAP 43

1. Apollo Ho. (D1)
2. Vane Cl. (B5–B6)
3. Flask Wlk. (A5– B5)
4. Spaniards [Road] (A3–B2); Carlingford Rd. (B5); Wedderburn [Road] (B6)
5. Ornan Rd. (C6) – if the middle letter 'n' in Ornan is replaced by a 'g', the word becomes organ
6. Tasker Rd. (D6) – if the third letter 's' is replaced by 'n', it forms the word 'tanker'
7. Kenwood House (C2) – originally built in the early part of the 17th century, it was later converted to a neoclassical villa. It was home to the Earl of Iveagh, whose art collection was bequeathed to the nation. Since 1929, it has been open to the public and its collection includes Rembrandt's masterpiece *Self-Portrait with Two Circles*
8. Keats Ho. (C5) – this is a museum and literary centre dedicated to the English Romantic poet John Keats (1795–1821). Keats lived in the house for a short period in 1818 before moving to Rome, where he died of tuberculosis
9. Compton Av. (C1) – Denis Compton (1918–97) was a distinguished sportsman of the 1940s and 1950s who played football and cricket at an elite level. In cricket, he earned 78 caps for England, while at football his team won the League title in 1948 and the FA Cup in 1950

MAP 44

1. The following 12/13 trees can be found:
   a) Acacia: Acacia Ct. (C2) b) Beech: Beechwood (B1)/Copper Beeches (B3)
   c) Cedar: The Cedars/Cedar Gdns. (A1/B1) d) Elder: Elder Pl. (D5)
   e) Elm: Elm Ct. (B4)/Elms Lea Av. (B1/B2) f) Holly: Holly Cl. (B1)
   g) Oak: Oak Close (B1) h) Pine: The Pines (B6) (also Pinewood (A1–B1) and Pinewood Close (A2–B2)) i) Poplar: Poplar Cl. (C2) j) Robinia: Robinia Lodge (B2) k) Silver birch: Silver Birches (B3) l) Walnut: Walnut Cl. (B1)
   m) Also, cut off on the left-hand side of the map, is Willow: Willow Ct. (A5)
2. Rugby Road (D3)
3. Denmark Terrace (B6)
4. Merlin Cl. (A4)
5. Seven Dials (C5)
6. St. Ann's Well Gardens (A5/B5)
7. Providence Place (D5) – Providence is the capital of Rhode Island, which is nicknamed 'The Ocean State' to draw attention to its coastline along the Atlantic Ocean
8. Osmond Road (B5–B6) – the Osmond Brothers came to prominence in the early 1970s, and their song *Love Me For A Reason* spent three weeks at number 1 in August 1974
9. Preston Park (B3/C3) – the Wellesbourne is a winter-flowing river which runs beneath the park

MAP 45

1. Nightingale Cl. (A6) and Robins [Wood Road] (B1)
2. Abbots Wy. (B3–C3)
3. Triumph Road (D2–D4)
4. Varden Av. (A6) – if you change the first letter to 'g', it forms the word 'garden'
5. Radford Bridge Road (C1–C2) – if the first vowel is changed from 'a' to 'e', you get the surname of the US actor Robert Redford, noted for his role in the Western *Butch Cassidy and the Sundance Kid*
6. Spean Ct. (A2) – if the last letter 'n' is changed to 'r', it forms the word 'spear'
7. DH Lawrence Pavilion (C6) – David Herbert (DH) Lawrence (1885–1930) was a noted English novelist and poet whose book, *Lady Chatterley's Lover*, privately published in 1928, recounted the story of a woman's love affair across the classes with a gamekeeper. It was not allowed to be published until 1960 due to the frank way in which the relationship was depicted
8. Loach Ct. (C2) – Ken Loach is known for films including *Kes* (1969), *The Wind That Shakes The Barley* (2006) and *I, Daniel Blake* (2016). He is one of a small number of directors to have won the Palme D'Or at Cannes twice
9. Gaynor Ct. (B1) – Gloria Gaynor is an American singer who is best known for her disco era hits such as *I Will Survive*, *Never Can Say Goodbye*, *Let Me Know* and *I Am What I Am*

MAP 46

1. There are 10 in total, located in the green areas : D1, 2 in B2, 3 in B3, D3, D5, C6, D6
2. Battery Cl. (A5)
3. Calvados Cl. (A6) – Calvados is named after the Calvados department in Normandy
4. a) Lidderdale Rd. (C1); b) Harringay Av. (D2); c) Gladstone, in 'Roscoe & Gladstone Hall' (C3)
5. Ullet Wk. (Walk) (B2) – if the letter 'm' is put in front, it spells 'mullet'
6. Otterspool (A6)/Otterspool Road (B6–B5) – it sounds like 'otters pool'
7. Rankin Hall (C5) – Ian Rankin is a Scottish crime writer noted for his Inspector Rebus novels, set primarily in Edinburgh. His first Rebus novel, *Knots and Crosses*, was published in 1987
8. Milner Road (C6–C5) – James Milner earned sixty-one caps for England before retiring from international football in 2016. His Twitter handle, @BoringMilner, plays on his image for giving bland responses in interviews
9. Sefton Park Palm House (B3/B4) – among its many plants, it includes over twenty species of palm

MAP 47

1. Brow Cl. and Brow Cr. (D5)
2. Holly Rd. (D3)
3. Maple Ct. (D2) – the maple leaf appears on the Canadian flag
4. Oakland Dr. (C1)
5. Elim Gro. (C5) – if you reverse the word, you form the word 'mile'
6. a) Gatesbield Ho. (C3); b) Orrest Dr./ Orrest Dr. Flats (D3)
7. Whinfield Rd. (D4) – if the letter 'n' is changed to 't', it forms 'Whitfield', the surname of the actress Dame June Whitfield, noted for her roles in classic sitcoms such as *Terry and June* and *Absolutely Fabulous*
8. Spooner Vale (C2) – William Archibald Spooner (1844–1930) was an Anglican clergyman and long-serving Oxford don, noted for sometimes transposing the initial letters of words – he once said 'weight of rages' instead of 'rate of wages', for example
9. Thornhill (D4) – Sir James Thornhill (1675–1734) was an English baroque painter best known for his work decorating the dome of St Paul's Cathedral
10. Queen Adelaide's Hill (B2) – it was named after Queen Adelaide, widow of King William IV and the aunt of Queen Victoria, after she visited the site in 1840. Prior to this visit it was known as Rayrigg Bank

MAP 48

1. Silver Ct. (D2) ('silver' can also be found at the start of Silverdale Terrace (C2))
2. Cyprus Gdns. (D4)
3. Harrison Gds. (A3) – George Harrison was a member of the Beatles
4. Draught's Garden (B3) – 'checkers' is the US name for the game of draughts
5. Sourmilk Hill La. (D4) – as in 'sour' and 'milk'
6. Alderley Rd. (B5) – if the sixth letter, 'l', is changed to 'n', it becomes Alderney, the northernmost of Britain's inhabited Channel Islands
7. Saltwell Towers Visitors Centre (B4/C4) – Saltwell Towers is a mansion built in 1862 by William Wailes, and is surrounded by ornamental gardens
8. Warburton Cres. (C2) – Sam Warburton overtook the record of 33 caps previously held by Ryan Jones in March 2015
9. Betjeman M. (Mews) (C1) – John Betjeman was succeeded by Ted Hughes in 1984

MAP 49

1. Monday Cr. /Monday Pl. (B6)
2. Holland Drive/Holland Park (B5)
3. Powys Pl. (A6)
4. Montagu Avenue (A1)/Montagu Ct. (A2) – if you add an 'e' it becomes Montague, the surname of Romeo in Shakespeare's *Romeo and Juliet*
5. Race Hill (B3) – where you could 'race' (compete) against Damon Hill, who won the Formula One championship in 1996
6. Avolon Ct./Avolon Pl. (B6) – if the second vowel 'o' is replaced by an 'a', it forms 'Avalon'
7. St. James' Park (C6) – home of Newcastle United, one end of the ground is called the Gallowgate End, named after the city's gallows that were last used in 1844
8. Forsyth [Road] (D3) – Bruce Forsyth presented family entertainment shows such as *The Generation Game*, *The Price Is Right* and *Strictly Come Dancing*. He died in 2017 after a showbusiness career spanning more than seventy years
9. Leazes Park (C6) – it was created, after a petition of working men, out of a part of Leazes Town Moor

MAP 50

1. Horse Wynd (A2), along with Whinny Hill (C2)
2. Earth: Dynamic Earth (A2)
3. Paisley Crescent, Paisley Gds. and Paisley Ter. (D2)
4. Blacket Av./Blacket Pl. (A5) – if the second letter is changed to 'r', it forms the word 'bracket'
5. Scone Gs. (Gardens) (D1)
6. Prestonfield (C6)/Prestonfield House (C5)/Prestonfield Golf Course (C5)/ Prestonfield Avenue (B6-C6)/Prestonfield Ter. (B6)/Prestonfield Gds. (B6) – it can be split into 'p rest on field', with the 'p' taken to mean 'quiet' per its usage in music
7. Arthur's Seat (B4/C4) – the name is believed to be a corruption of a Gaelic term for 'height of arrows', which over the years became transformed into the much more atmospheric 'Arthur's Seat'
8. Burns Monument (A2) – it commemorates Scotland's foremost poet and lyricist, Robert Burns (1759–96). Designed by the architect Thomas Hamilton, it was built between 1831 and 1839
9. Montrose Ter. (A1) – Montrose is 38 miles north of Dundee and the northernmost town in the county of Angus. William Wallace destroyed its castle after it had sworn allegiance to King Edward I of England, the 'Hammer of the Scots'

Bonus Quiz

Churchill:
Map 9, Churchill Park (A1); Map 16, Churchill Rd. (B6); Map 18, Churchill Villas (D3), Churchill Way (D2–D3); Map 20, Churchill Cr. (C5); Map 23, Churchill War Rooms (B6); Map 36, Churchill St. (A2)

Jubilee:
Map 2, Jubilee Yd. (C6); Map 3, The Jubilee (A3); Map 22, Jubilee Cr. (A5); Map 32, Golden Jubilee Bridges (A3), Jubilee Gardens (A3); Map 35, Jubilee Ter. (C6); Map 37, Jubilee Trade Centre (D6)

Springfield
Map 13, Springfield Rd. (C5/D5); Map 17, Springfield Cl. (D6); Map 19, Springfield Gdns. (C4–C3), Springfield Road (C4–C3), Springfield Rd. (A5–C4); Map 26, Springfield Cl. (D6), Springfield Cottages (D6), Springfield House (C6); Map 29, Springfield Road (B1); Map 44, Springfield Road (C4–D4), written as 'Spring Field' across an A-road); Map 48, Springfield Pl. (D4); Map 49, Springfield Ho. (B1)

Orchard
Map 3, The Orchard (C5/D5), Orchard Dr. (5C), Orchard Hill (A5–A4), Orchard Rd. (D5); Map 4, Orchard Cl. (B6), Orchard M. (C6); Map 7, Orchard Cl. (B1–B2); Map 8, Orchard St. (D3); Map 13, Rectory Orchard (B4); Map 15, Apple Orchard (C3); Map 16, Orchard Business Park (B3), Smiths Orchard (D4); Map 21, Orchard St. (A3); Map 22, Orchard Pl. (C2); Map 25, The Orchard (C6), The Orchard Primary School (D5); Map 26, Cherry Orchard (A4–B4), Holly Orchard (C1), Orchard Way (A3–B3); Map 28, Orchard Cl. (B6); Map 39, Orchard Sq. (A2, close to the fold), Orchard Sq. Shopping Centre (A2), Orchard St. (A2, may be hidden in the fold of the book); Map 41, Orchard St. (D2); Map 42, Orchard Rd. (D6); Map 46, The Orchard (D6); Map 48, Orchard Gdns. (D6)

Victoria:

Map 1, Queen Victoria Memorial (C3), Victoria Place Shopping Centre (B6), Victoria Square (B4), Victoria Station (Rail & Underground) (B6/B5), Victoria [Street] (B5–D5), Queen Victoria Memorial Gdns. (C2–C3); Map 3, Victoria Pde. (A2); Map 4, Victorian Grove (D3–D2); Map 8, Victoria St. (D4); Map 10, Victoria St. (D4), Victoria Ter. (C4), Victoria St. (D4); Map 11, Victoria Avenue (D5–D4), Victoria Ct. (C5); Map 13, Victoria Drive (A1–B2); Map 15, Victoria Ho. (A4/B4); Map 16, Queen Victoria St. (D4), Victoria Av. (A3, near the fold); Map 18, Victoria Pl. (C3); Map 23, Queen Victoria Memorial (A6), Victoria Embankment (C6–D4); Map 26, Victoria Cl. (C2); Map 27, Victoria Buildings (C4); Map 29, Queen Victoria Rd. (C4–D5), Victoria St. (B2); Map 34, Queen Victoria Memorial (C1), Victoria Coach Station (A5, near the fold), Victoria Place Shopping Centre (B4), Victoria Square (B2), Victoria Station (Rail & Underground) (B4/B3), Victoria [Street] (B3–D3); Map 35, Victoria Av. (C6), Victoria Road (A3–B3), Victoria Pier (B6), Victoria Park (C4); Map 36, Victoria Cr. (A3), Victoria Pk. (C3); Map 37, Victoria Sq. (A3), Victoria Sq. Stop (Metro) (A3); Map 39, Victoria Quays (D1); Map 41, Victoria & Albert Museum (A6/B6), Victoria Gate (A3/B3); Map 42, Victoria Cotts. (C4), Victoria Ga. (C4); Map 44, Victoria Place (B6, shown as Via. P.), Victoria Rd. (B6), Victoria St. (B6); Map 46, Victoria Cl. (C4), Victoria Rd. (C4); Map 47, Victoria St. (D2); Map 49, Queen Victoria Rd. (D6–D5), Royal Victoria Infirmary (C5/D6)

ACKNOWLEDGEMENTS

Many thanks to Steve Berger, Steve Egleton, Jennie Fraser, Mark McConnell, Matt Trigg and all at A-Z Maps for the fabulously detailed street maps of the whole of the country.

Also to Henry Bell for his encylopedic knowledge of British history, Karen Midgley for her meticulous checking and editorial skills, and Jethro Lennox, Clare Souza and Lauren Murray at HarperCollins Publishers for guiding the book through the whole process.

Gareth also wishes to thank his wife, Sara, for her continuing support.

AS THE FACE OF LONDON CHANGES, A-Z MAPS HAS CAPTURED IT ALL.

For the last century, A-Z Maps has been the trusted and reliable source of mapping for Londoners.
Through archived maps and interesting stories, Philip Parker reveals how the city has changed over the last one hundred years.

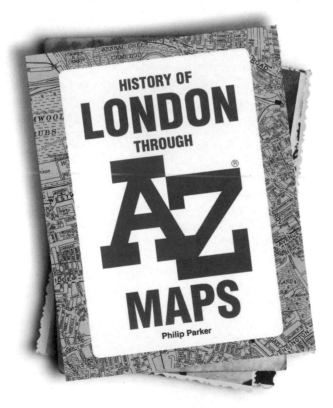

AVAILABLE ONLINE AND AT ALL GOOD BOOKSHOPS

3.10.19